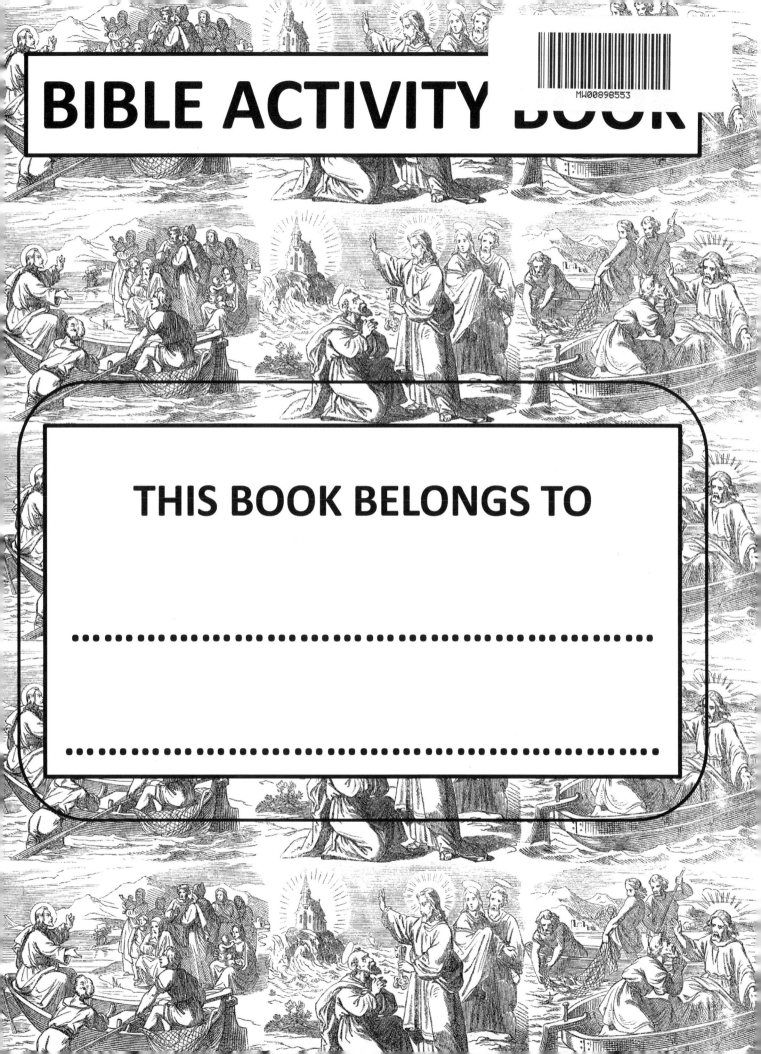

BIBLE ACTIVITY BOOK

THIS BOOK BELONGS TO

....

....

MW00898553

BIBLE ACTIVITY BOOK

Copyright © 2021, **Michael Obi Press** All rights reserved. No part of this publication may be reproduced or transmitted in any form or by any means, electronic or mechanical, including photocopy, recording, or any information storage and retrieval system, without permission in writing from the publisher.

INTRODUCTION

This bible activity book contains word search puzzles, crossword puzzles, cryptogram, word scramble and Sudoku puzzles. All the puzzles in this book are created using bible theme. The book is created to entertains kids and also help them grow in the knowledge of the scripture. It contains a perfect mixture of easy and hard puzzles that is appropriate for kids between the ages of 8 to 12. The solution to each puzzle is also provided at the end of each puzzle type, to help kids out when they get stocked.

WHY PUZZLE FOR KIDS?

- Puzzles help kids improve their memory, planning skills, and problem-solving aptitude.

- The experience of solving a puzzle can also teach your kids to embrace difficulties, find solutions, and handle frustration.

- Kids who solve puzzles have better attention spans, which allows them to focus better and be more patient when completing tasks.

- When kids finish a puzzle, they can check another accomplishment off their list, gain confidence in their skills, and feel better about themselves.

TABLE OF CONTENTS

WELCOME
TO
WORD SEARCH
PUZZLES

HOW TO SOLVE

Find all the word capitalized words listed below the puzzles on each page. Words are hidden in the grids of the puzzle in straight, unbroken lines: forward, backwards, up, down or diagonal. Words can over lap and cross each other. When you find a word, circle it in the grid and mark the word in the list so you will know it has been found. Each words should be searched for as individual word.

FOODS IN BIBLE

```
A H O N E Y B Q C F M R
I K M V C V I N E G A R
K O O F H Y L S G Y N F
N Z L B E W F M G S N I
I M G L E H W L S X A S
R E R U S E M E O M P H
E A B R E A D G I U Y P
B T U L U T X R O S R H
E S T E W S W S E T K N
S A T M M I L K A A N U
H W E H B O A I I R V J
T R R P Z C O R N D R F
```

BREAD   FLOUR WHEAT   FISH   BUTTER CAKES

CHEESE STEWS MUSTARD VINEGAR   CORN MEATS

BARLEY SOUPS   MILK EGGS HONEY MANNA

SPICES AND HERBS IN BIBLE

```
Q C M P C D X L P S O B
B R U E O X Q U W M P G
E Y S M R W G G H R O Q
S F T M I O Q A O Z G P
J X A U A N C R Y B O P
Z W R K N D I L L V K C
L V D J D V N I I S W D
I X O H E T N C K F Z K
M Y K E R S A L T N O V
I C K G H L M I N T H T
G P U R E U O G H J M A
A F R I E A N I S E K Z
```

CORIANDER   CINNAMON   CUMIN   ANISE   DILL

MUSTARD   GARLIC   MINT   RUE   SALT

FRUITS AND NUTS IN BIBLE

```
H Q X C V U F R I T O F
Q P I S T A C H I O X A
G B M L R W D A T E S P
R S C S S M S I R N R P
Z A P V Q G W O G U E L
G V R B I R M J L M G E
K F C F H A L M O N D S
Q O Q A C P J E O N F K
I M R Y Z E O L I V E S
I S S Z K S Z O A Z G I
P O M E G R A N A T E S
E W E P R A I S I N S J
```

APPLES ALMONDS DATES FIGS GRAPES

MELONS OLIVES PISTACHIO POMEGRANATES

RAISINS   SYCAMORE

RIVERS AND SEAS IN THE BIBLE 1

```
W R P S R E K Z G R A S
G R P W B G I H O N E S
T T C R P L S B Z T I C
O B J U W A A B A N A S
E C B W Q H M R N O X W
V H M E Q A H A V A J P
R E I C R P C U N O T A
Q R M H U M G D I A M E
N I L E Q U P C H C P S
F T N B V W Y Q N Z B C
R H U A W Z O G D S O P
K J A R N O N K O K Q W
```

ABANA   AHAVA   AMANA   ARNON

NILE   CHEBAR   CHERITH   EUPHRATES

GIHON   GOZAN   HABOR

RIVERS AND SEAS IN THE BIBLE 2

```
I  X  F  A  S  H  I  H  O  R  K  N
D  V  P  H  P  M  A  U  L  A  I  M
R  D  S  Z  B  E  P  H  S  P  S  C
P  E  L  E  G  J  W  I  I  K  H  T
G  I  T  N  T  A  K  D  H  W  O  M
J  R  S  R  J  R  K  D  O  Q  N  Z
X  K  A  O  T  K  K  E  R  C  W  E
I  A  T  A  N  O  Z  K  B  A  F  D
V  N  R  N  B  N  W  E  K  V  H  E
X  A  E  B  Y  H  Z  L  R  J  L  T
P  H  A  R  P  A  R  U  F  E  I  V
I  J  O  R  D  A  N  T  B  A  D  E
```

PARAT   HIDDEKEL   JABBOK   JORDAN

KANAH   KISHON   MEJARKON   PELEG PHARPAR

PISON   SHIHOR   SIHOR   ULAI   ZERED

MEN IN THE BIBLE

```
A J J H M J Y L D S D X
G B C K E M G N Y P Q B
Z P R G F S A M U E L S
D T H A Z U I T F X W X
F Y C I H E U T T G P H
M U Z S L A Z Y G H H Y
R D O A T I M R N H E P
G J H A K D P B A T G W
E M I C H A E L T L U N
Z E C H A R I A H F B I
X M B M T R Z I A P F G
H L V K I E L P N H Q X
```

NATHAN ISAAC MATTHEW EZRA

ZECHARIAH SAMUEL PHILIP

JOSHUA ABRAHAM MICHAEL

MEN IN THE BIBLE 2

```
D  A  N  I  E  L  P  Z  M  C  A  M
R  N  I  T  N  H  K  V  V  A  A  U
B  S  G  L  S  O  P  E  T  E  R  R
K  Z  C  I  Z  D  A  V  I  N  O  K
V  M  W  T  J  T  U  F  S  Q  N  I
T  I  H  C  E  X  L  J  C  F  H  H
Z  S  T  A  R  T  I  M  O  T  H  Y
U  A  Z  N  E  L  I  J  A  H  T  I
Y  I  N  D  M  C  U  N  B  F  N  Z
G  A  B  R  I  E  L  K  Z  D  R  Z
M  H  H  E  A  M  O  S  E  S  Q  N
Q  P  D  W  H  E  S  Z  Y  J  U  L
```

AARON DANIEL ELIJAH GABRIEL ISAIAH

JEREMIAH LUKE MARK MOSES PETER

ANDREW DAVI JOHN PAUL TIMOTHY

WOMEN IN THE BIBLE

```
S T T W A A Z F S P U S
C N Y N L U S M O F W W
M X Q S V M E X C D Y M
M I R I A M S D N Z R P
V A Y W O P T X V P K R
S B G S Y D H G W M W A
X J C D J H E K F S R C
O E A V A V R B R U T H
A L C C E L Q Q O J A E
I G O C B I E M A R Y L
C L E E H A N N A H A X
C Z G Q P P G S E O N H
```

MARY   RUTH   MAGDALENE   RACHEL

HANNAH   EVE   DEBORAH

ESTHER   MIRIAM   SARAH

WOMEN IN THE BIBLE 2

```
W Q P U U Y N G L C S Y
U S R F R Q J P B L V U
Z J I Q J J E R A H A B
P Q S P K E H X T G J Q
K G C R X Z O I H V A G
D P I B E E S P S T P Q
B E L S P B H G H M M Z
S J L F Q E E M E A A K
F I A I X L B K B R V O
V I I J L M A H A T J U
O E L I Z A B E T H F F
T J Q L E A H B T A N Y
```

ELIZABETH   PRISCILLA   MARTHA   JEHOSHEBA

REBEKAH   LEAH   RAHAB

DELILAH   BATHSHEBA   JEZEBEL

TREES IN THE BIBLE

```
R  W  W  A  L  M  U  G  Q  K  B  Y
V  N  G  G  U  Q  W  D  E  A  O  O
O  Y  W  G  L  I  O  A  D  H  S  K
O  S  L  G  R  S  R  B  C  K  W  J
C  A  B  C  X  U  I  B  E  J  E  Y
T  L  L  A  F  I  V  H  U  R  L  C
W  O  M  M  L  Q  D  W  T  I  L  A
J  E  D  P  O  M  A  C  A  C  I  A
H  S  O  H  O  N  Z  P  V  B  A  T
Q  L  S  I  R  D  D  N  P  K  E  F
C  A  J  R  C  C  T  K  L  L  Z  P
V  O  L  E  H  M  I  O  U  Y  E  X
```

ACACIA ALGUM ALMOND ALMUG

ALOES   APPLE ASH

BALM BOSWELLIA CAMPHIRE

TREES IN THE BIBLE 2

```
Q B B B R R M C K J L D
G V N U I G M I Q G N Q
S O V T I O M N A A K H
Z Q Z J M O X N B V O R
L W Q L F D M A H Y F N
H S D C E L H M N N C X
N F H A E Y J O E L K Y
D E Q S T D B N V D I L
K V S S G E A W F W Y K
N A H I C Y P R E S S N
S R F A D R D W M Y R T
L J F B X M G P M B E V
```

CASSIA   CEDAR   CINNAMON

CYPRESS   DATE   EBONY

ELM   FIG   GOODLY

TREES IN THE BIBLE 3

```
L Y H H K Z O E G X X X
N S E A N X V V V O F O U
O O A M Z P G J P L O D
K K T P U E H R H Z T H
F R H L K L L S E O K Q
X X I X V J B G R A F T
B B M Y R T L E N K A N
T E Y W S X P Z R K K U
N I R P V I S U P R Q E
T E R B N E Y R I B Y O
S U H U I J B H E G O L
M T J M Z H P C P H M E
```

GOPHER GRAFT HAZEL

HEATH JUNIPER MULBERRY

MYRRH MYRTLE OAK

TREES IN THE BIBLE 4

T	E	I	L	T	R	E	E	X	W	P	G
L	O	K	L	O	K	J	Z	Z	U	O	R
Q	X	W	X	V	E	H	D	O	M	M	P
S	Y	C	A	M	I	N	E	T	R	E	E
O	F	U	G	P	O	P	L	A	R	G	S
T	E	R	E	B	I	N	T	H	C	R	Y
R	J	T	H	O	R	N	D	U	Q	A	C
P	A	L	M	T	R	E	E	N	N	N	A
J	W	F	G	K	R	I	F	T	Y	A	M
Y	N	S	A	F	W	I	C	T	R	T	O
O	I	P	L	A	N	E	T	R	E	E	R
R	L	G	S	F	Q	F	O	L	I	V	E

OLIVE PALMTREE PINETREE PLANETREE

POMEGRANATE POPLAR SYCAMINETREE TOW

SYCAMORE TEILTREE TEREBINTH THORND

ANIMALS IN THE BIBLE

```
V H O H T Y W P Z Z C O
R B Y D H A B O C R N X
S P C W U U P S A I A U
N C F Z P B E E L D C P
I J I K Q W B R D F O M
U M S Z W W E A W C R L
L Y E E H F H L T A I R
L N B T S S E E U C C S
K Q N G H X M V B O G I
D A N T E L O P E M T Q
D L O C U S T K F D D K
L R W W A H H L A G R C
```

ADDAX   ANT   ANTELOPE

APE   LOCUST   BAT

BEAR   BEE   BEHEMOTH

ANIMALS IN THE BIBLE 2

```
L  G  C  M  F  J  V  O  K  T  X  N
N  B  S  A  K  B  W  K  V  F  C  Q
B  C  O  R  M  O  R  A  N  T  K  G
B  P  E  O  J  B  N  O  B  S  S  B
G  C  N  D  Z  U  E  C  S  I  T  U
X  M  Y  H  X  L  C  A  M  E  L  Z
V  J  Q  R  E  C  R  G  K  G  D  Z
L  L  U  M  D  U  Y  C  O  B  R  A
G  F  A  N  M  A  I  D  R  Z  A  R
U  H  H  N  S  R  K  B  E  A  C  D
C  O  W  T  C  T  O  M  Y  E  N  E
T  U  Y  R  Y  V  V  O  U  Q  R  E
```

BUZZARD CAMEL CHAMELEON COBRA

CORMORANT COW CRANE

ASS CRICKET DEER DOG

ANIMALS IN THE BIBLE 3

```
I  U  X  R  C  C  E  V  Y  P  L  G
O  J  O  R  N  W  R  U  X  L  Y  R
F  R  Q  H  T  B  O  L  N  V  J  A
G  A  B  A  C  L  U  T  E  V  M  S
D  O  N  K  E  Y  J  U  L  X  D  S
U  G  A  F  F  C  S  R  F  I  S  H
U  E  Z  R  G  A  Z  E  L  L  E  O
S  C  A  O  Y  T  L  H  E  R  W  P
I  K  X  G  Z  M  Q  C  A  E  Q  P
D  O  V  E  L  P  N  O  O  J  P  E
F  L  Y  O  K  E  L  X  T  N  N  R
R  K  I  L  O  U  K  P  Y  M  C  W
```

DONKEY DOVE EAGLE VULTURE FALCON

FISH FLEA FLY FOX FROG

GAZELLE GECKO GNAT GOA GRASSHOPPER

ANGELS IN THE BIBLE

```
J Q F L T M Q O T L Q C
T Y D M G T E J L P G K
G J E R E M I E L P R F
O W J D H H I G Z S C X
A G C X A M C U Q A J O
B P Z A A R J D X F Q L
T I A R M Z I I J Q T O
X U F P E A I E C B V F
M Z H A N I E L L W B Y
F J O P H I E L A S N B
F B A R A C H I E L F Z
E N W O Q R D N J N I E
```

JOPHIEL   JEGUDIEL   HANIEL   BARACHIEL

ARIEL RAMIEL JEREMIEL CAMAEL

ANGELS IN THE BIBLE 2

I	B	T	W	J	Y	S	L	O	M	P	T
X	L	A	Z	R	A	E	L	R	U	H	H
U	P	A	L	J	I	A	M	Q	K	A	V
H	R	Y	H	R	A	L	L	X	B	N	W
D	T	I	B	P	E	T	U	Z	V	U	X
V	R	A	E	I	M	I	C	H	A	E	L
E	G	R	K	L	I	E	I	O	O	L	V
G	G	D	X	S	B	L	F	O	Q	S	V
R	A	P	H	A	E	L	E	P	B	M	N
Z	T	V	P	J	A	N	R	P	Q	D	W
S	Y	J	U	I	G	S	E	C	W	A	A
R	J	H	V	M	G	K	Y	Z	Y	I	K

PHANUEL   ZADKIEL   AZRAEL

URIEL   RAPHAEL   MICHAEL

GABRIEL LUCIFER SEALTIEL

KINGS IN THE BIBLE

```
G B K V N R N Z O S F A
R E H O B O A M J T O D
U A Z U M H T H B G G A
Y C Q O A K S F P R S V
C O L U D A A E R C L I
P O L E O X U U K I D D
S P F H N F L Z S G R I
M M E U I X F Z I Z T L
H J C W J A D I L O P X
S P A M A Z I A H J J P
E J O T H A M H W Y V M
L F N J A J P B Z G M T
```

SAUL DAVID ADONIJAH SOLOMON

REHOBOAM JEHOASH AMAZIAH

UZZIAH JOTHAM AHAZ

KINGS IN THE BIBLE 2

```
L  J  U  F  F  D  R  J  I  C  P  W
M  M  A  N  A  S  S  E  H  I  Z  K
H  E  Z  E  K  I  A  H  Y  S  X  B
A  D  F  E  Z  F  A  O  H  R  X  F
O  V  K  C  D  I  N  I  Q  B  J  J
D  J  O  B  S  E  Z  A  M  O  N  F
S  A  L  O  X  G  K  K  P  B  F  W
P  U  J  E  C  O  N  I  A  H  B  F
J  O  X  O  G  M  U  M  A  G  F  T
Z  S  X  A  J  E  H  O  A  H  A  Z
O  O  N  M  Z  D  A  H  F  W  T  R
Q  M  Q  N  N  S  O  V  A  U  F  V
```

HEZEKIAH MANASSEH AMON JOSIAH

JEHOAHAZ JEHOIAKIM JECONIAH ZEDEKIAH

KINGS IN THE BIBLE 3

```
P B E L S H A Z Z A R R
U O R W H H M F X N T A
J A Q X A R A J C C C X
Z R X K L P A R N U V S
I T T U M T C D G H U B
B A P D A V M I F I B F
I X Y N N V X O R Z N C
J E K X E P U A J Y R A
J R S K S O D U A Y F I
W X P F E H P U S X R C
R E C Y R U S M R X G J
Q S E N N A C H E R I B
```

PUL SHALMANESER SHARGINA SENNACHERIB

BELSHAZZAR CYRUS DARIUS ARTAXERXES

CHURCHES IN THE BIBLE

```
F  A  H  P  I  H  W  H  U  P  F  E
D  L  M  Q  J  M  I  M  Q  H  S  B
O  A  T  T  U  W  U  I  C  I  C  B
A  O  Q  E  F  M  M  P  N  Q  L  A
L  D  I  K  A  I  T  H  P  A  U  G
G  I  A  G  W  Z  H  E  X  D  D  O
J  C  R  R  L  G  Y  P  M  E  T  Z
E  E  V  X  T  P  A  H  A  L  Y  W
P  A  C  S  L  O  T  E  E  P  J  Q
F  L  S  A  R  D  I  S  D  H  A  P
C  C  E  L  D  M  R  U  P  I  V  Y
B  S  M  Y  R  N  A  S  K  A  O  B
```

EPHESUS SMYRNA PERGAMUM THYATIRA

SARDIS PHILADELPHIA LAODICEA

PROPHETS IN THE BIBLE

P	C	G	R	E	G	A	P	F	W	R	R
K	X	A	F	Q	D	M	N	H	S	H	R
F	T	D	I	E	N	K	H	G	M	L	M
V	P	V	R	N	O	T	M	U	A	A	F
L	N	A	B	O	E	N	O	C	H	M	Y
F	J	O	R	S	Q	N	J	Q	A	E	B
J	Y	H	A	F	I	A	U	X	L	C	V
V	M	E	T	H	U	S	E	L	A	H	U
X	O	K	M	N	T	Z	O	T	L	Q	A
E	X	F	M	D	S	H	W	Q	E	J	R
Q	V	V	W	E	X	L	B	S	E	A	Q
A	I	X	R	L	R	Y	Q	V	L	W	K

SETH ENOS CAINEN MAHALALEEL

JARED ENOCH METHUSELAH

LAMECH NOAH NOE

PROPHETS IN THE BIBLE 2

```
U B P S Q A E M G Y U C
I M E L C H I Z E D E K
H I Y J X C B S K D J R
P J F R E P H R A I M T
S E O V U R R Q R A J T
F T E S Z X E Q A U C O
O Z L O E D B M Z D E M
F E I D K P J K I A N Y
G L A B R A H A M A H L
E G S H E M C M C R H X
P S D C E U C O D O A G
D P R E S Q F L M Z B J
```

SHEM   MELCHIZEDEK   ABRAHAM   ISAAC

JACOB   JOSEPH   EPHRAIM

ELIAS   GAD   JEREMIAH

PROPHETS IN THE BIBLE 3

```
S C X R J A H A Z I E L
Q S A U V R M O S E S J
F W C Y I E K H B X U H
W Q E V T F A M E O M Z
M Z W L B J E E K D J Z
D A N W I Z M L Q U O X
D T S H V S C I I S S K
Q R A N K E H J T H H W
L C M Y L F W A H V U F
J I U U N A T H A N A S
Z E E D X E V U G S R A
J K L U V H Y O S H N O
```

ELIHU   MOSES   JOSHUA   EXODUS

SAMUEL   NATHAN   AHIJAH

JAHAZIEL   ELIJAH   ELISHA

PROPHETS IN THE BIBLE 4

```
C E X Q A A H D Y V X J
I U A H B Z W W N H F D
F S I A R W C F L Z D A
B Q A Q W H A G G A I N
R Q O I M O T L Z I W I
D U J E A S U P O H H E
H I O L Z H V Y B C X L
Y O N E H E M I A H P S
J E A F A A K L D Y O M
V U H R H E A I I M K K
K I Z I J M T V A F X M
Z E C H A R I A H L X X
```

JONAH   AMOS   HOSHEA   ISAIAH

OBADIAH   EZEKIAL   DANIEL ZECHARIAH

HAGGAI EZRA NEHEMIAH MALACHI

MOUNTAINS IN THE BIBLE

```
C J S L A A K H K B B K
D F E P H R A I M M J V
O A K B Z S A O I M M H
O A S L A N Q R R W X T
Y G G I L E A D A F S A
N H O R E B G Z L T I B
A S Z E A A E U R I N O
O L I V E S R T K B A R
G P O A K H I Z H S I I
N Q N X L A Z X Z E R W
X L J O G N I G S D L P
A B Z Z A J M O R I A H
```

ABARIM ARARAT BASHAN BETHEL EBA

EPHRAIM GERIZIM GILEAD HOREB SINAI

MORIAH OLIVES SEIR TABOR ZION

BIRDS IN THE BIBLE

```
A C X J P E P E S M K V H Q
F V W S C W N I W C L Y
Z T R Y U J Q I L J K Z
W O A X L V F T L U C L
H S V P I G U L L Q Z O
K S E A E A G L E K O E
J I N S I V W X T R S A
Z F T K W O G X C U T G
H R U E M W H U W A R L
V A Q R U W C A Z Q I E
J G W K I V V F Z S C B
P E B K F X B J N O H R
```

EAGLE   OSSIFRAGE   SEAEAGLE

VULTURE   KITE   RAVEN

OSTRICH OWL   GULL   HAWK

BIRDS IN THE BIBLE 2

```
E F U M X G V S S S W A N
N T D Y C H H T A H B I
H O O P O E F Z S C F G
P Y I T R T W I R I Y H
R G P M M J B P X U V T
C M J P O I M M H E C R
L W F E R T G Z P E Y A
P W E L A E M Y L N B V
F G U I N E A F O W L E
U L S C T R U R V J K N
K H B A T K E W E Q W D
L A O N R H K U R C F K
```

NIGHTRAVEN CORMORANT SWAN

IBIS PELICAN PLOVER HERON

HOOPOE BAT GUINEAFOWL

PLACES IN THE BIBLE

```
J O R D A N U N I U J N
W B B Z R P E D J D B Z
E J E Z I D O X W S F D
M Z T U E O C A N A A N
I L H S L G N I N T Q P
T U A Y J A U M K G N B
H Y N A E L H I A R Q V
D Q Y O R I X V L X I J
M X S H I L O H V N C J
S N H F C E G O N E Q J
R X F M H A R I T C N J
C C S X O I A M D X I S
```

EDEN   ZION   JORDAN   SHILOH

JERICHO   BETHANY   ARIEL

CANAAN   GALILEA   BEULAH

FOODS IN BIBLE

```
A H O N E Y B Q C F M R
I K M V C V I N E G A R
K O O F H Y L S G Y N F
N Z L B E W F M G S N I
I M G L E H W L S X A S
R E R U S E M E O M P H
E A B R E A D G I U Y P
B T U L U T X R O S R H
E S T E W S W S E T K N
S A T M M I L K A A N U
H W E H B O A I I R V J
T R R P Z C O R N D R F
```

SPICES AND HERBS IN BIBLE

```
Q C M P C D X L P S O B
B R U E O X Q U W M P G
E Y S M R W G G H R O Q
S F T M I O Q A O Z G P
J X A U A N C R Y B O P
Z W R K N D I L L V K C
L V D J D V N I I S W D
I X O H E T N C F Z K D
M Y K E R S A L T N O V
I C K G H L M I N T H T
G P U R E U O G H J M A
A F R I E A N I S E K Z
```

FRUITS AND NUTS IN BIBLE

```
H Q X C V U F R I T O F
Q P I S T A C H I O X A
G B M L R W D A T E S P
R S C S S M S I R N R P
Z A P V Q G W O G U E L
G V R B I R M J L M G E
K F C F H A L M O N D S
Q O Q A C P J E O N F K
I M R Y Z E O L I V E S
I S S Z K S Z O A Z G I
P O M E G R A N A T E S
E W E P R A I S I N S J
```

REIVERS AND SEAS IN THE BIBLE

```
W R P S R E K Z G R A S
G R P W B G I H O N E S
T T C R P L S B Z T I C
O B J U W A A B A N A S
E C B W Q H M R N O X W
V H M E Q A H A V A J P
R E I C R P C U N O T A
Q R M H U M G D I A M E
N I L E Q U P C H C P S
F T N B V D V W Y Q N Z
R H U A W Z O G D S O P
K J A R N O N K O K Q W
```

REIVERS AND SEAS IN THE BIBLE 2

```
I X F A S H I H O R K N
D V P H P M A U L A I M
R D S Z B E P H S P S C
P E L E G J W I I K H T
G I T N T A K D H W O M
J R S R J R K D O Q N Z
X K A O T K K E R C W E
I A T A N O Z K B A F E
V N R N B N W E K V H E
X A E B Y H Z L R J L T
P H A R P A R U F E I V
I J O R D A N T B A D E
```

MEN IN THE BIBLE

```
A J J H M J Y L D S D X
G B C K E M G N Y P Q B
Z P R G F S A M U E L S
D T H A Z U I T F S W W
F Y C I H E U T T G P H
M U Z S L A Z Y G H H J
R D O A T I M R N H E P
G J H A K D P B A T G W
E M I C H A E L T L U N
Z E C H A R I A H F B I
X M B M T R Z I A P F G
H L V K I E L P N H Q X
```

MEN IN THE BIBLE 2

```
D A N I E L P Z M C A M
R N I T N H K V V A A U
B S G L S O P E T E R R
K Z C I Z D A V I N O K
V M W T J T U F S Q N I
T I H C E X L J C F H H
Z S T A R T I M O T H Y
U A Z N E L I J A H T I
Y I N D M C U N B F N Z
G A B R I E L K Z D R Z
M H H E A M O S E S Q N
Q P D W H E S Z Y J U L
```

WOMEN IN THE BIBLE

```
S T T W A A Z F S P U S
C N Y N L U S M O F W W
M X Q S V M E X C D Y M
M I R I A M S D N Z R P
V A Y W O P T X V P K R
S B G S Y D H G M W D U
X J C D J H E K F S R C
O E A V A V R B R U T H
A L C C E L Q Q O J A E
I G O C B I E M A R Y L
C L E E H A N N A H A X
C Z G Q P P G S E O N H
```

WOMEN IN THE BIBLE 2

```
W Q P U U Y N G L C S Y
U S R F R Q J P B L V U
Z J I Q J J E R A H A B
P Q S P K E H X T G J Q
K G C R X Z O I H V A G
D P I B E E S P S T P Q
B E L S P B H G H M M Z
S J L F Q E E M E A A K
F I A I X L B K B R V O
V I I J L M A H A T J U
O E L I Z A B E T H F F
T J Q L E A H B T A N Y
```

TREES IN THE BIBLE

```
R W W A L M U G Q K B Y
V N G G U Q W D E A O O
O Y W G L I O A D H S K
O S L G R S R B C K W J
C A B C X U I B E J E Y
T L L A F I V H U R L C
W O M M L Q D W T I L A
J E D P O M A C A C I A
H S O H O N Z P V B A T
Q L S I R D D N P K E F
C A J R C C T K L L Z P
V O L E H M I O U Y E X
```

TREES IN THE BIBLE 2

```
Q B B B R R M C K J L D
G V N U I G M I Q G N Q
S O V T I O M N A A K H
Z Q Z J M O X N B V O R
L W Q L F D M A H Y F N
H S D C E L H M N N C X
N F H A E Y J O E L K Y
D E Q S T D B N V D I L
K V K S S G E A W F W K
N A H I C Y P R E S S N
S R F A D R D W M Y R T
L J L F B X M G M 2 B E V
```

TREES IN THE BIBLE 3

```
L Y H H K Z O E G X X X
N S E A N X V V O F O U
O O A M Z P G J P L O D
K K T P U E H R H Z T H
F R H L K L U S E O K Q
X X I X V J B G R A F T
B B M Y R T L E N K A N
T E Y W S X P Z R K H U
N I R P V L S U P R Q E
T E R B N E Y R I B Y O
S U H U I J B H E G O L
M T J M Z H P C P H M E
```

TREES IN THE BIBLE 4

```
T E I L T R E E X W P G
L O K L O K J Z Z U O R
Q X W X V E H D O M M P
S Y C A M I N E T R E E
O F U G P O P L A R G S
T E R E B I N T H C R Y
R J T H O R N D U Q A C
P A L M T R E E N N N A
J W F G K R I F T Y A M
Y N S A F W I C T R T O
O I P L A N E T R E E R
R L G S F Q F O L I V E
```

ANIMALS IN THE BIBLE

```
V H O H T Y W P Z Z C O
R B Y D H A B O C R N X
S P C W U U P S A I A U
N C F Z P B E E L D C P
I J I K Q W B R D F O M
U M S Z W W E A W C R L
L Y E E H F H L T A I R
L N B T S S E E U C C S
K Q N G H X M V B O G I
D A N T E L O P E M T Q
D L O C U S T K F D D K
L R W W A H H L A G R C
```

ANIMALS IN THE BIBLE 2

```
L G C M F J V O K T X N
N B S A K B W K V F C Q
B C O R M O R A N T K G
B P E O J B N O B S S B
G C N D Z U E C S I T U
X M Y H X L C A M E L Z
V J Q R E C R G K G D Z
L L U M D U Y C O B R A
G F A N M A I D R Z A R
U H H N S R K B E A C D
C O W T C T O M Y E N E
T U Y R Y V V O U Q R E
```

ANIMALS IN THE BIBLE 3

```
I U X R C C E V Y P L G
O J O R N W R U X L Y R
F R Q H T B O L N V J A
G A B A C L U T E V M S
D O N K E Y J U L X D S
U G A F F C S R F I S H
U E Z R G A Z E L L E O
S C A O Y T L H E R W P
I K X G Z M Q C A E Q P
D O V E L P N O O J P E
F L Y O K E L X T N N R
R K I L O U K P Y M C W
```

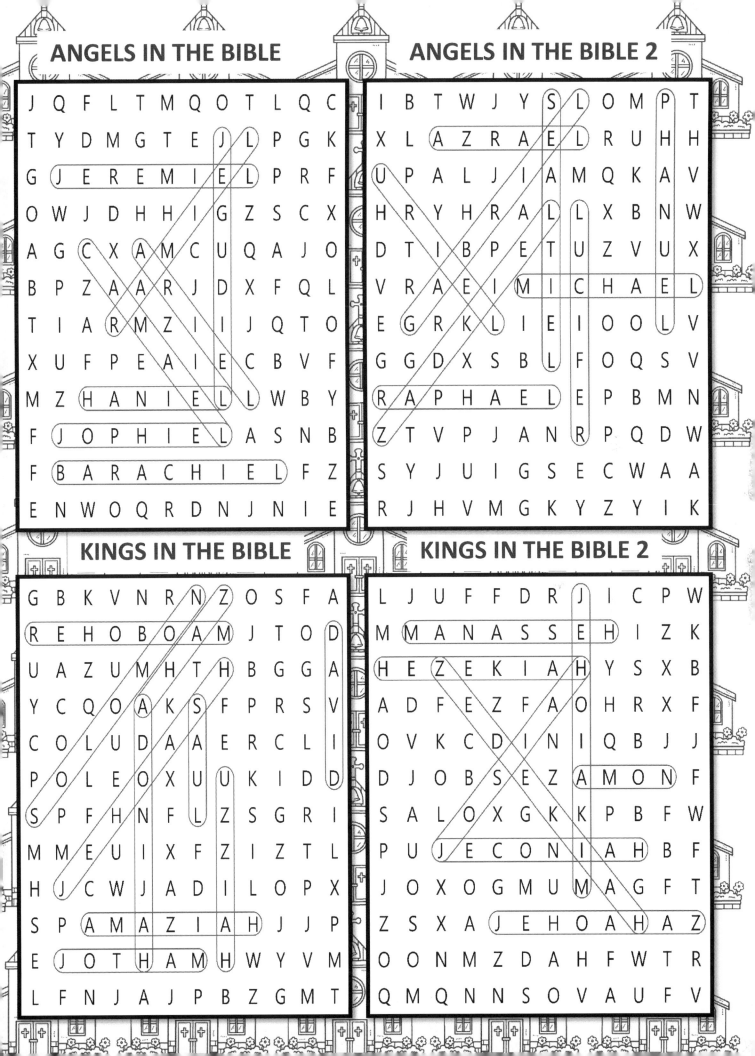

KINGS IN THE BIBLE 3

```
P B E L S H A Z Z A R R
U O R W H H M F X N T A
J A Q X A R A J C C C X
Z R X K L P A R N U V S
I T T U M T C D G H U B
B A P D A V M I F I B F
I X Y N V X O R Z N C
J E K X E P U A J Y R A
J R S K S O D U A Y F I
W X P F E H P U S X R C
R E C Y R U S M R X G J
Q S E N N A C H E R I B
```

CHURCHES IN THE BIBLE

```
F A H P I H W H U P F E
D L M Q J M I M Q H S E
O A T T U W U I C I B K
A O Q E F M P N Q L A U
L D I K A I T H P A U G
G I A G W Z H E X D D O
J C R R L G Y P M E T Z
E E V X T P A H A L Y W
P A C S L O T E E E P J
F L S A R D I S D H A P
C C E L D M R U P I V Y
B S M Y R N A S K A O B
```

PROPHETS IN THE BIBLE

```
P C G R E G A P F W R R
K X A F Q D M N H S H R
F T D I E N K H G M L M
V P V R N O T M U A A F
L N A B O E N O C H M Y
F J O R S Q N J Q A E B
J Y H A F I A U X L C V
V M E T H U S E L A H U
X O K M N T Z O T L Q A
E X F M D H X L B S E A
Q V V W E X L B S E A Q
A I X R L R Y Q V L W K
```

PROPHETS IN THE BIBLE 2

```
U B P S Q A E M G Y U C
I M E L C H I Z E D E K
H I Y J X C B S K D J R
P J F R E P H R A I M T
S E O V U R R Q R A J T
F T E S Z X E Q A U C O
O Z L O E D B M Z D E M
F E I D K P J K I A N Y
G L A B R A H A M A H L
E G S H E M C M C R H X
P S D C E U C O D O A G
D P R E S Q F L M Z B J
```

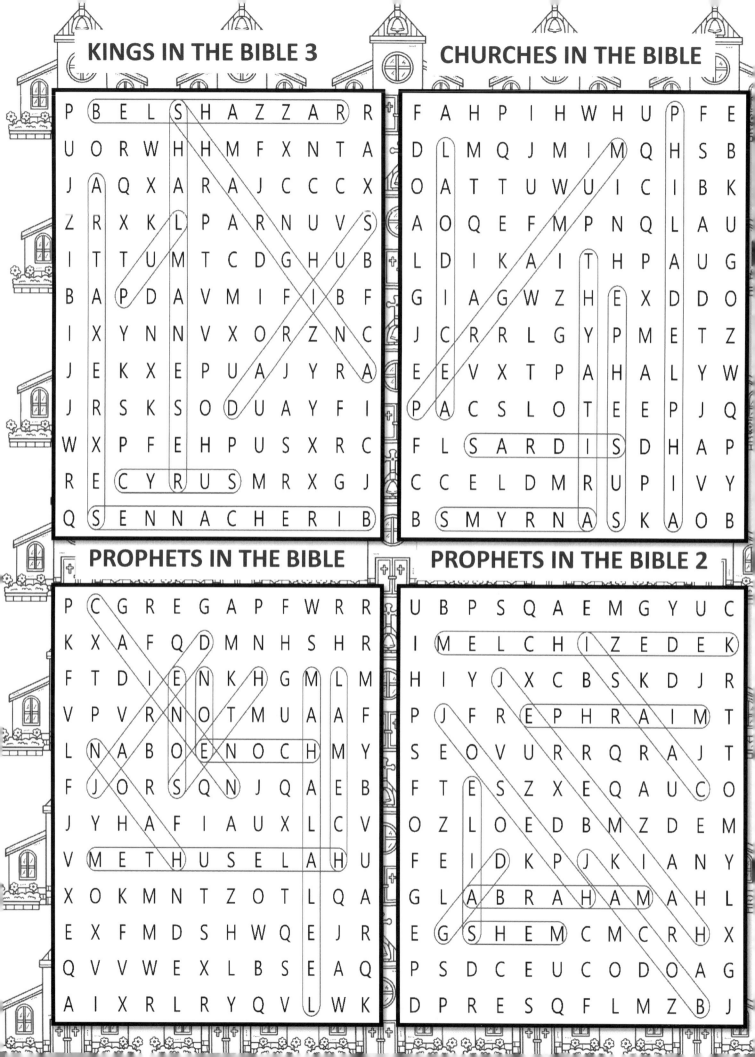

PROPHETS IN THE BIBLE 3

```
S C X R J A H A Z I E L
Q S A U V R M O S E S J
F W C Y I E K H B X U H
W Q E V T F A M E O M Z
M Z W L B J E E K D J Z
D A N W I Z M L Q U O X
D T S H V S C I I S S K
Q R A N K E H J T H H W
L C M Y L F W A H V U F
J I U U N A T H A N A S
Z E E D X E V U G S R A
J K L U V H Y O S H N O
```

PROPHETS IN THE BIBLE 4

```
C E X Q A A H D Y V X J
I U A H B Z W M N H F D
F S I A R W C F L Z D A
B Q A Q W H A G G A I N
R Q O I M O T L Z I W I
D U J E A S U P O H H E
H I O L Z H V Y B C X L
Y O N E H E M I A H P S
J E A F A A K L D Y O M
V U H R H E A I I M K K
K I Z I J M T V A F X M
Z E C H A R I A H L X X
```

MOUNTAINS IN THE BIBLE

```
C J S L A A K H K B B K
D F E P H R A I M M J V
O A K B Z S A O I M M H
O A S L A N Q R W X X T
Y G G I L E A D A F S A
N H O R E B G Z L T I B
A S Z E A A E U R I N O
O L I V E S R T K B A R
G P O A K H I Z H S I I
N Q N X L A Z X Z E R W
X L J O G N I G S D L P
A B Z Z A J M O R I A H
```

BIRDS IN THE BIBLE

```
A C X J P E S M K V H Q
F V W S C W N I W C L Y
Z T R Y U J Q I L J K Z
W O A X L V F T L U C L
H S V P I G U L L Q Z O
K S E A E A G L E K O E
J I N S I V W X T R S A
Z F T K W O G X C U T G
H R U E M W H U W A R L
V A Q R U W C A Z Q I E
J G W K I V F E X S C B
P E B K F X B J N O H R
```

BIRDS IN THE BIBLE 2

E	F	U	M	X	G	V	S	S	W	A	N
N	T	D	Y	C	H	H	T	A	H	B	I
H	O	O	P	O	E	F	Z	S	C	F	G
P	Y	I	T	R	T	W	I	R	I	Y	H
R	G	P	M	M	J	B	P	X	U	V	T
C	M	J	P	O	I	M	M	H	E	C	R
L	W	F	E	R	T	G	Z	P	E	Y	A
P	W	E	L	A	E	M	Y	L	N	B	V
F	G	U	I	N	E	A	F	O	W	L	E
U	L	S	C	T	R	U	R	V	J	K	N
K	H	B	A	T	K	E	W	E	Q	W	D
L	A	O	N	R	H	K	U	R	C	F	K

PLACES IN THE BIBLE

J	O	R	D	A	N	U	N	I	U	J	N
W	B	B	Z	R	P	E	D	J	D	B	Z
E	J	E	Z	I	D	O	X	W	S	F	D
M	Z	T	U	E	O	C	A	N	A	A	N
I	L	H	S	L	G	N	I	N	T	Q	P
T	U	A	Y	J	A	U	M	K	G	N	B
H	Y	N	A	E	L	H	I	A	R	Q	V
D	Q	Y	O	R	I	X	V	L	X	I	J
M	X	S	H	I	L	O	H	V	N	C	J
S	N	H	F	C	E	G	O	N	E	Q	J
R	X	F	M	H	A	R	I	T	C	N	J
C	C	S	X	O	I	A	M	D	X	I	S

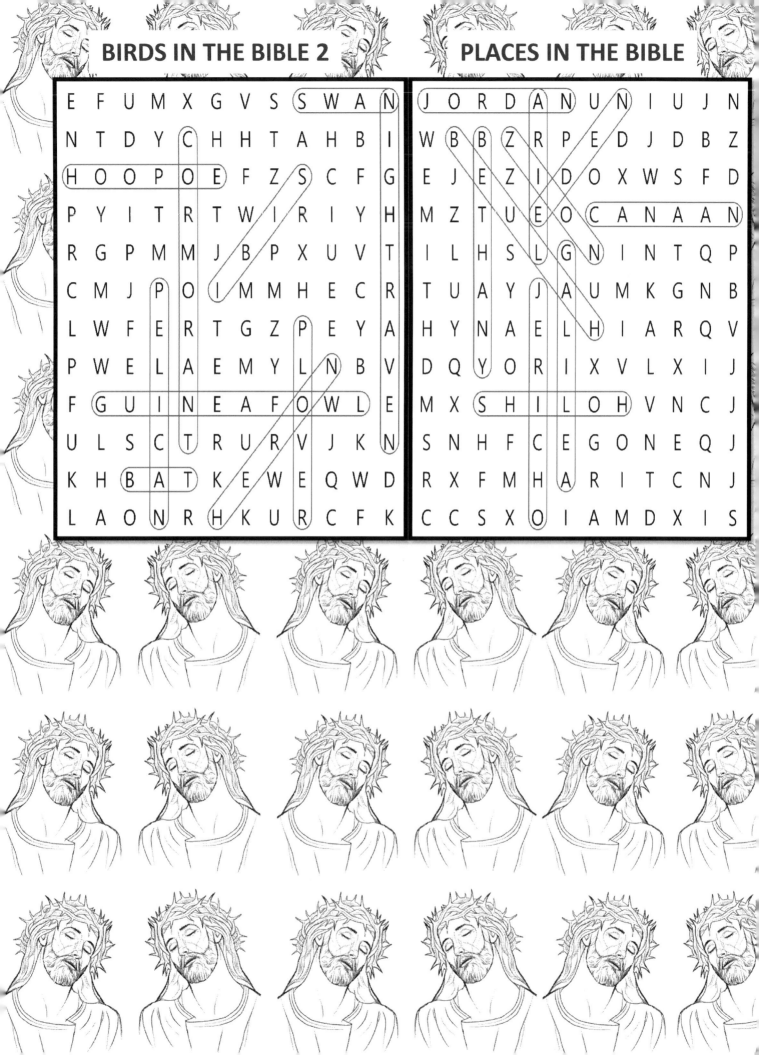

WELCOME TO CROSSWORD PUZZLES

Tips for Solving Crossword Puzzles

- Work with pencil
- Go over the clues for any 3, 4 and 5 letter words.
- Enter any guessed answers in the box with a pencil.

PUZZLE 1

Across

3. The human author that wrote the most books of the bible.

4. The insect John the Baptist ate in the desert.

6. The first book of the bible.

9. The apostle that disowned Jesus three times, after he was arrested.

10. The book of the bible Jesus wrote.

Down

1. The longest book in the Bible.

2. The island Paul was shipwrecked on.

5. The city was Jesus born.

7. The person that recognized Jesus as the Messiah when he was presented at the Temple as a baby.

8. The language most of the Old Testament was first written in.

PUZZLE 2

Across

4. In every battle you will need faith as your _____ to stop the fiery arrows aimed at you by Satan.

6. The first person to come upon the injured man in the parable of the Good Samaritan.

8. Matthew was a _____.

10. The number of days it took God to create the world.

11. The day God rested.

Down

1. The city Saul was traveling to when he encountered a great and blinding light?

2. For _____so love the world that he gave his only begotten son.

3. The last book of the bible.

5. The most likely first Gospel written.

7. The author of the Book of Revelation.

9. The human author that wrote the most words in the Bible.

PUZZLE 3

Across

3. Paul's name before he started his missionary work.

5. The person God told to build an ark

7. Simon Peter's occupation before he becomes an apostle.

8. The number of baskets left over after Jesus fed 5,000+ people with two fish and five loaves of bread.

10. The day God created man.

Down

1. The angel that told Virgin Mary she was pregnant.

2. The person Paul said Christians should follow his example in Chapter 5 of Ephesians.

4. The first man God created.

6. Paul's tribe.

9. The first women God created.

PUZZLE 4

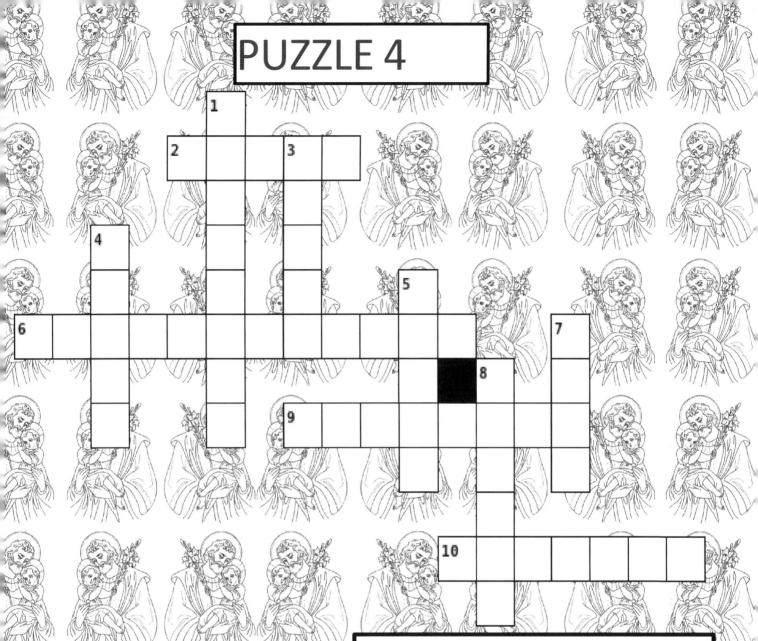

Across

2. The name of the tower men were trying to build to reach heaven.

6. The person the killed John the Baptist.

9. The high priest of Jerusalem that put Jesus on trial.

10. God's sign to Noah he would never destroy the earth with water again.

Down

1. What God used in confusing men building tower to heaven.

3. The number of people saved in Noah's ark.

4. The numbers of day and night it rained when Noah was on the ark.

5. Name of Abraham's wife.

7. The sign Judas used in betraying Jesus.

8. The apostle that doubted Jesus's resurrection.

PUZZLE 5

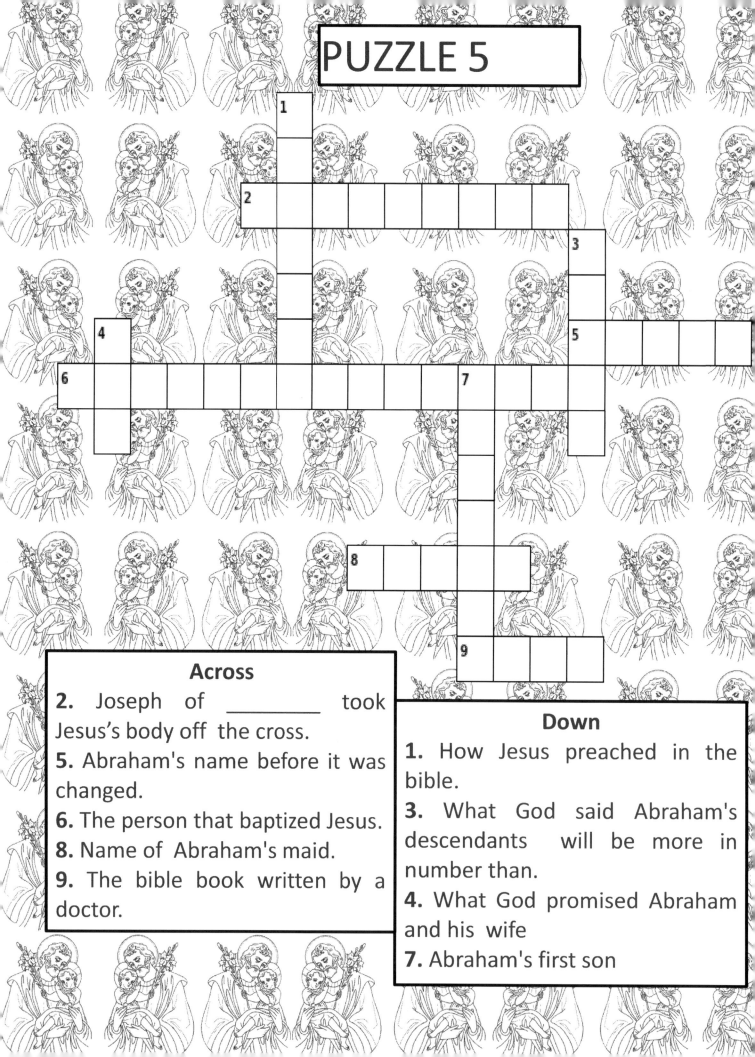

Across

2. Joseph of _____ took Jesus's body off the cross.

5. Abraham's name before it was changed.

6. The person that baptized Jesus.

8. Name of Abraham's maid.

9. The bible book written by a doctor.

Down

1. How Jesus preached in the bible.

3. What God said Abraham's descendants will be more in number than.

4. What God promised Abraham and his wife

7. Abraham's first son

PUZZLE 6

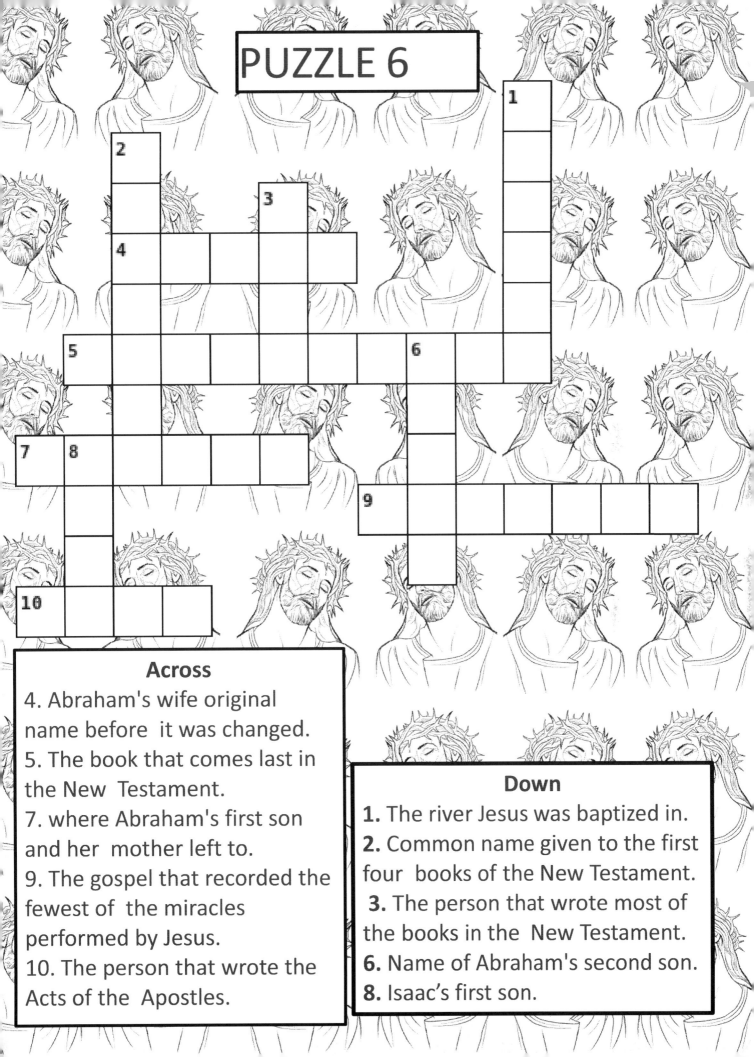

Across
4. Abraham's wife original name before it was changed.
5. The book that comes last in the New Testament.
7. where Abraham's first son and her mother left to.
9. The gospel that recorded the fewest of the miracles performed by Jesus.
10. The person that wrote the Acts of the Apostles.

Down
1. The river Jesus was baptized in.
2. Common name given to the first four books of the New Testament.
3. The person that wrote most of the books in the New Testament.
6. Name of Abraham's second son.
8. Isaac's first son.

PUZZLE 7

Across

2. Laban trick Jacob into marrying_____?

5. What Esau did for a living.

7. The name of the place Jesus was crucified.

8. How many brothers did Joseph have?

9._____was taken from Esau by his brother?

10. Number of years Jacob worked for Laban to finally marry Rachel.

Down

1. The tax collector that climbed up a tree so he could see Jesus.

3. Water was turned into _____at the marriage in Cana.

4. Number of days Jesus appear to his disciples after his resurrection.

6. The city Paul and Silas were imprisoned during the second missionary journey.

PUZZLE 8

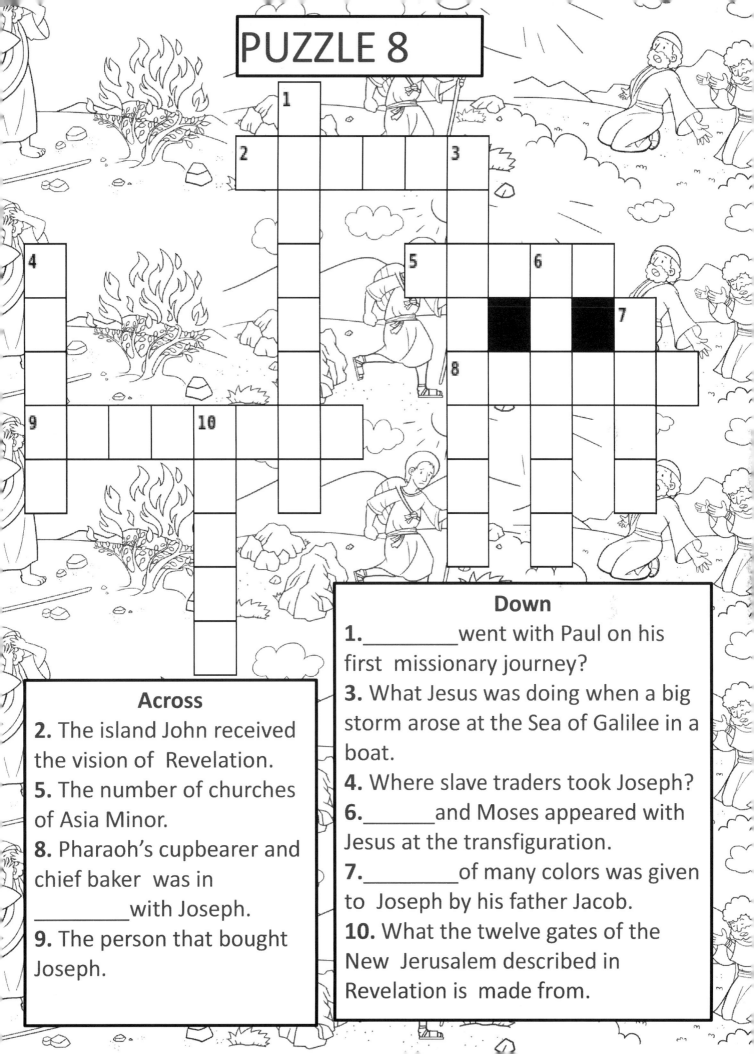

Across

2. The island John received the vision of Revelation.
5. The number of churches of Asia Minor.
8. Pharaoh's cupbearer and chief baker was in _____ with Joseph.
9. The person that bought Joseph.

Down

1. _____went with Paul on his first missionary journey?
3. What Jesus was doing when a big storm arose at the Sea of Galilee in a boat.
4. Where slave traders took Joseph?
6. _____and Moses appeared with Jesus at the transfiguration.
7. _____of many colors was given to Joseph by his father Jacob.
10. What the twelve gates of the New Jerusalem described in Revelation is made from.

PUZZLE 9

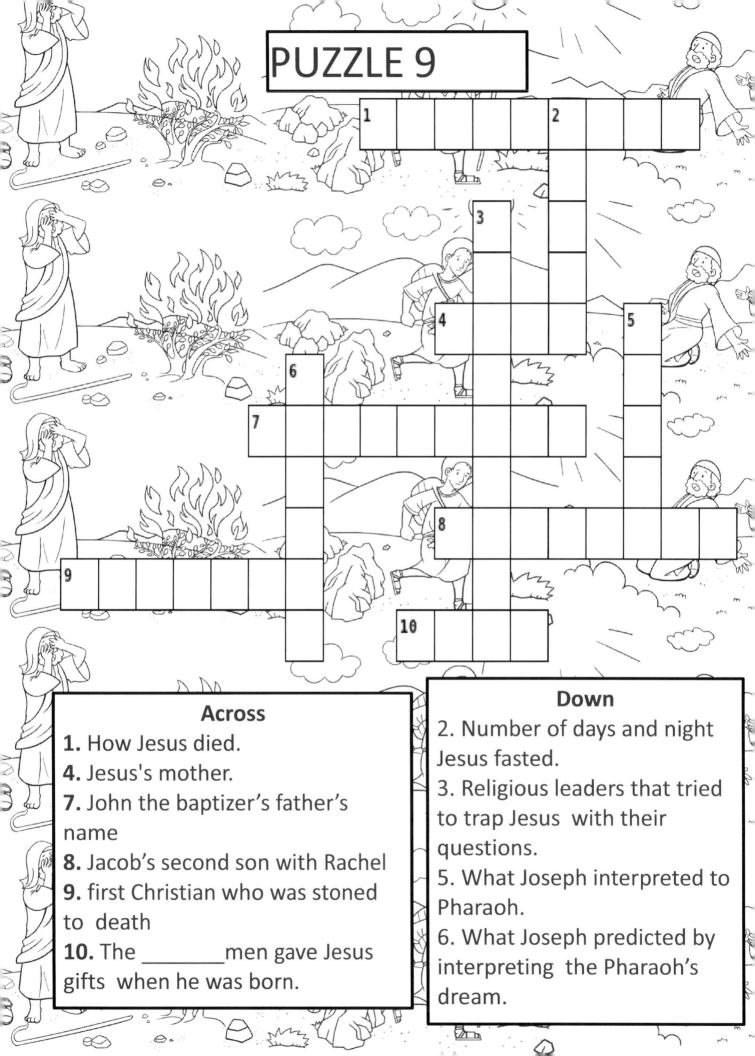

Across

1. How Jesus died.

4. Jesus's mother.

7. John the baptizer's father's name

8. Jacob's second son with Rachel

9. first Christian who was stoned to death

10. The _____men gave Jesus gifts when he was born.

Down

2. Number of days and night Jesus fasted.

3. Religious leaders that tried to trap Jesus with their questions.

5. What Joseph interpreted to Pharaoh.

6. What Joseph predicted by interpreting the Pharaoh's dream.

PUZZLE 10

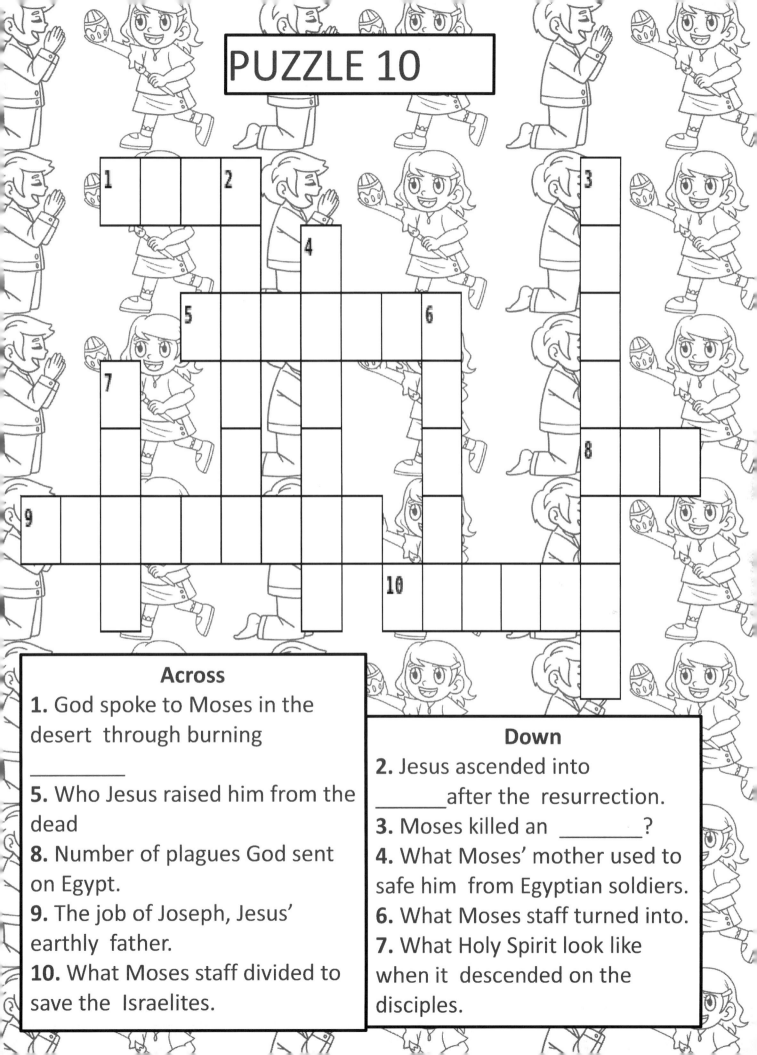

Across

1. God spoke to Moses in the desert through burning _____

5. Who Jesus raised him from the dead

8. Number of plagues God sent on Egypt.

9. The job of Joseph, Jesus' earthly father.

10. What Moses staff divided to save the Israelites.

Down

2. Jesus ascended into _____after the resurrection.

3. Moses killed an _____?

4. What Moses' mother used to safe him from Egyptian soldiers.

6. What Moses staff turned into.

7. What Holy Spirit look like when it descended on the disciples.

PUZZLE 11

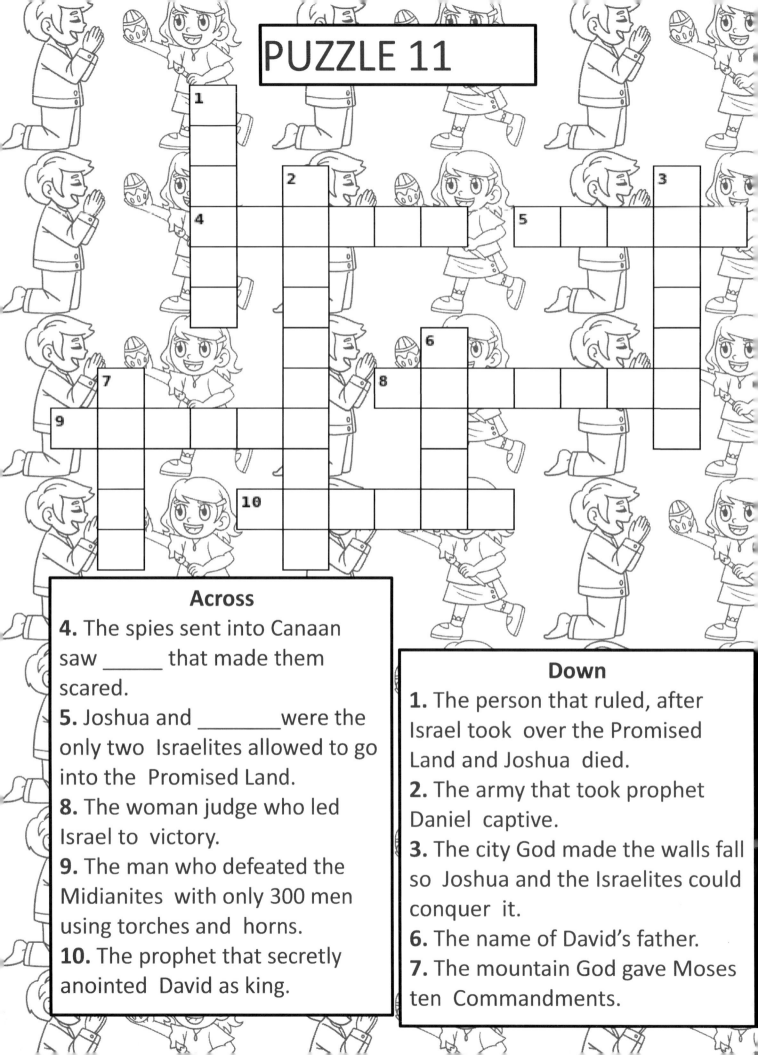

Across

4. The spies sent into Canaan saw _____ that made them scared.

5. Joshua and _____ were the only two Israelites allowed to go into the Promised Land.

8. The woman judge who led Israel to victory.

9. The man who defeated the Midianites with only 300 men using torches and horns.

10. The prophet that secretly anointed David as king.

Down

1. The person that ruled, after Israel took over the Promised Land and Joshua died.

2. The army that took prophet Daniel captive.

3. The city God made the walls fall so Joshua and the Israelites could conquer it.

6. The name of David's father.

7. The mountain God gave Moses ten Commandments.

PUZZLE 12

Across

4. _____ wanted the tribe of Judah to secede from the twelve tribes.

6. Samson died by pushing over the temple _____?

8. The man who took a Nazarite vow from birth and fought against the Philistines.

9. Object that Moses used to perform signs and wonders.

10. The women that betrayed Samson to the Philistines.

Down

1. The Israelites wandered the desert for forty _____.

2. Elijah's apprentice and successor.

3. _____ killed his brother Abel.

5. God feed the Israelites in the desert with bread-like substance from _____.

7. David brought   of the Covenant to Jerusalem to bless the religious city.

PUZZLE 13

Across

3. What King Solomon asked God for.

5. The name that means "mother of all living".

8. The women that promised to dedicate her son to God.

9. The women that remained with her mother-in-law, Naomi.

10. King _____ built a grand temple in Jerusalem.

Down

1. The women Abraham's servant found, when Looking for a wife for Isaac.

2. King Ahab's wife.

4. David's original wife.

6. The Jewish festival that resulted from the events in Esther.

7. Who wrote "The Lord is my Shepherd, I shall not want"?

PUZZLE 14

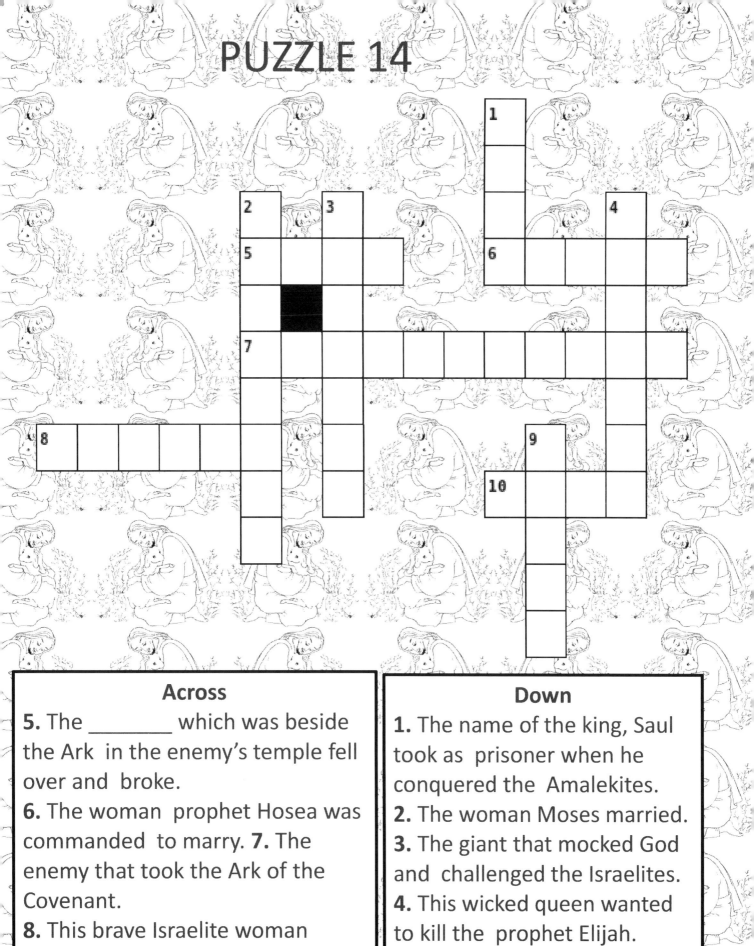

Across

5. The _____ which was beside the Ark in the enemy's temple fell over and broke.
6. The woman prophet Hosea was commanded to marry. **7.** The enemy that took the Ark of the Covenant.
8. This brave Israelite woman became queen of Persia
10. The first king of Israel.

Down

1. The name of the king, Saul took as prisoner when he conquered the Amalekites.
2. The woman Moses married.
3. The giant that mocked God and challenged the Israelites.
4. This wicked queen wanted to kill the prophet Elijah.
9. This king of Israel anointed by Samuel after Saul.

PUZZLE 15

Across

1. The commandment that told us to Honor our father and mother.
4. The men his wife was turned into a pillar of salt because she looked back.
6. Ruth's sister-in-law.
9. First thing that God created.
10. The number of sling-throws it took David to hit the giant.

Down

2. Number of each type of animal Noah had on the ark.
3. This woman gave birth to Moses.
5. The day God created plants.
7. What Saul try to give David to use in fighting the giant.
8. What David used to fight the giant.

PUZZLE 16

Across

3. The number of times David spared Saul's life.

7. The foreign country David run away to.

9. What did Saul throw to try to kill David?

10. Something that killed Saul.

Down

1. Who Saul turned to for advice when he couldn't sense God's will.

2. Saul's son that David befriended.

4. People look on the outward appearance, but God look in _____.

5. The food do we ask God to give us in the Lord's Prayer.

6. Moses' brother

8. Where David spared Saul's life the first time.

PUZZLE 17

Across
4. The prophet that came to rebuke David.
6. The Son of God.
7. Animal often used for transportation in the Bible.
10. The second child of Bathsheba.

Down
1. He was thrown into a lions' den by King Darius.
2. Jesus told a parable about a prodigal_____.
3. Bathsheba's husband.
5. David's son that started a rebellion against him
8. The prophet swallowed by a fish.
9. Commander of David's army.

PUZZLE 18

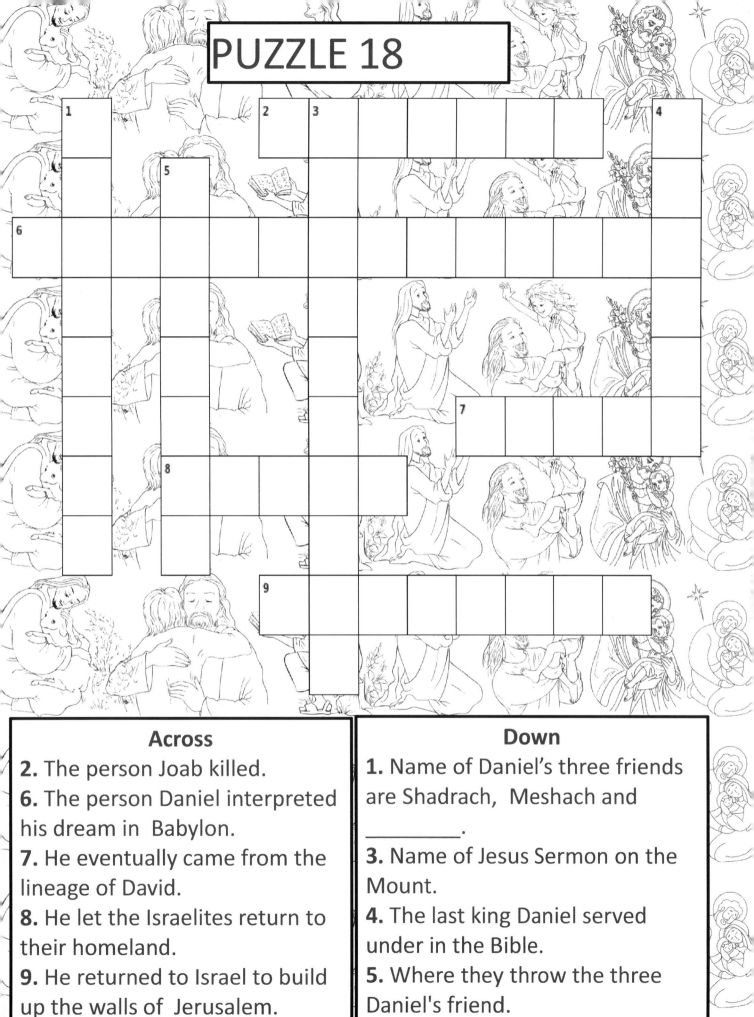

Across

2. The person Joab killed.

6. The person Daniel interpreted his dream in Babylon.

7. He eventually came from the lineage of David.

8. He let the Israelites return to their homeland.

9. He returned to Israel to build up the walls of Jerusalem.

Down

1. Name of Daniel's three friends are Shadrach, Meshach and _____.

3. Name of Jesus Sermon on the Mount.

4. The last king Daniel served under in the Bible.

5. Where they throw the three Daniel's friend.

PUZZLE 19

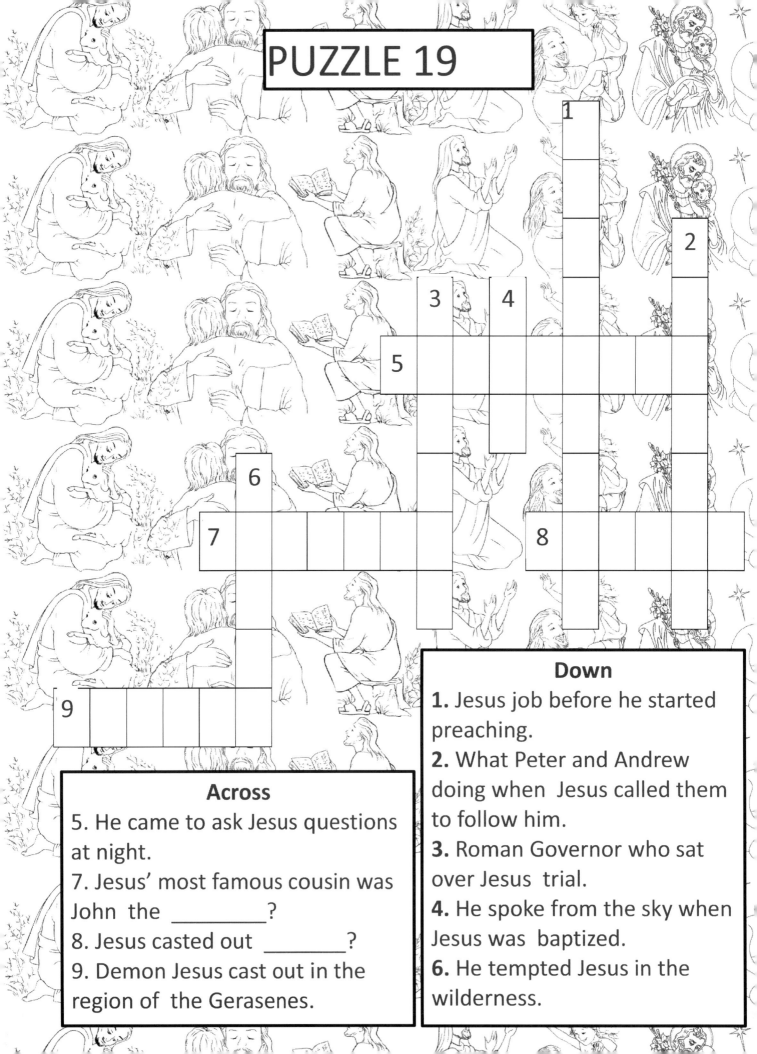

Across
5. He came to ask Jesus questions at night.
7. Jesus' most famous cousin was John the _____?
8. Jesus casted out _____?
9. Demon Jesus cast out in the region of the Gerasenes.

Down
1. Jesus job before he started preaching.
2. What Peter and Andrew doing when Jesus called them to follow him.
3. Roman Governor who sat over Jesus trial.
4. He spoke from the sky when Jesus was baptized.
6. He tempted Jesus in the wilderness.

PUZZLE 20

Across
2. He taught the Lord's Prayer.
6. He cut off a soldier's ear when Jesus was being arrested.
8. The Apostle that took the Gospel to the city of Samaria.
9. The 2 different kinds of birds Noah sent out from the Ark are _____ and Dove.

Down
1. He was crucified upside down.
3. First Christian to die for his faith.
4. The number of deacons chosen to help the apostles to distribute food to widows.
5. The number of Jesus's brothers named in the Bible.
7. He was in prison with Paul in Philippi when they were singing and there was an earthquake.

WELCOME
TO
CROSSWORD PUZZLES
SOLUTIONS

PUZZLE 1

1 PSALMS
2 MALTA
3 PAUL
4 LOCUSTS
5 BETHLEHEM
6 GENESIS
7 SIMEON
8 HEBREW
9 PETER
10 NONE

PUZZLE 2

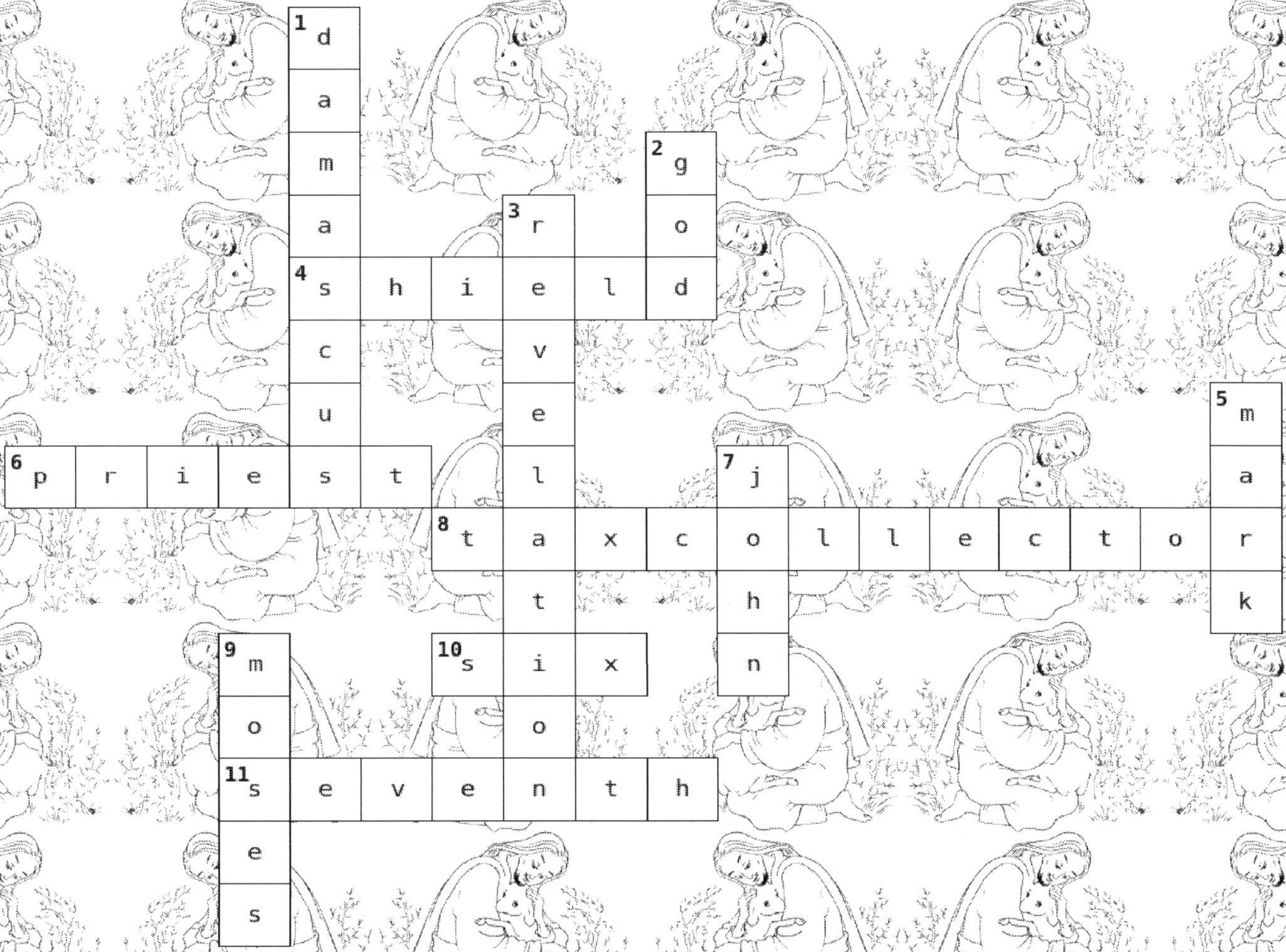
1 damascus
2 god
3 revelation
4 shield
5 mark
6 priest
7 john
8 taxcollector
9 moses
10 six
11 seventh

PUZZLE 3

			¹g										
²c		³s	a	u	l			⁴a			⁶b		
⁵n	o	a	h		b				d		e		
	h				r				a		n		
	r		⁷f	i	s	h	e	r	m	a	n		
	i			e						j			
	s		⁸t	w	e	l	v	⁹e			a		
								v			m		
								e		¹⁰s	i	x	t	h
										n			

PUZZLE 4

			¹L								
		²B	A	B	³E	L					
			N		I						
⁴F			G		G						
O			U		H		⁵S				
⁶H	E	R	O	D	A	N	T	I	P	A	S		⁷K
T			G		E			R	■	⁸T	I
Y			E			⁹C	A	I	A	P	H	A	S
						H			O		S
									M	
					¹⁰R	A	I	N	B	O	W
									S	

PUZZLE 5

Across:
- 2. ARIMATHEA
- 5. ABRAM
- 6. JOHNTHEBAPTIZER
- 8. HAGAR
- 9. LUKE

Down:
- 1. PARABLE
- 3. STARS
- 4. SON
- 7. ISHMAEL

PUZZLE 6

Across:
- 4. SARAI
- 5. REVELATION
- 7. DESERT
- 9. MATTHEW
- 10. LUKE

Down:
- 1. JORDAN
- 2. GOSPEL
- 3. PAUL
- 6. ISAAC
- 8. ESSA

PUZZLE 7

Across:
- 2. LEAH
- 5. HUNTING
- 7. GOLGOTHA
- 8. ELEVEN
- 9. BIRTHRIGHT
- 10. SEVEN

Down:
- 1. ZACCHAEUS
- 3. WINN
- 4. FORTY
- 6. PHILIPPI

PUZZLE 8

Across:
- 2. PATMOS
- 5. SEVEN
- 8. PRISON
- 9. POTIPHAR

Down:
- 1. BARNABAS
- 3. SLEEPING
- 4. EGYPT
- 6. ELIJAH
- 7. CONAT
- 10. PEARL

PUZZLE 9

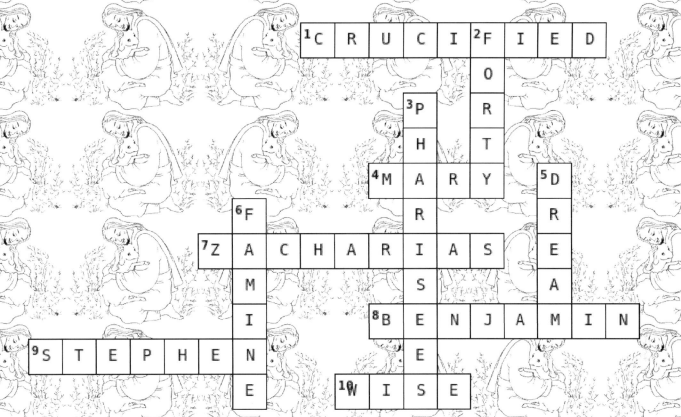

	¹C	R	U	C	I	²F	I	E	D

²F O R T Y

³P H

⁴M A R Y

⁵D R E A M

⁶F

⁷Z A C H A R I A S

⁸B E N J A M I N

⁹S T E P H E N E

¹⁰W I S E

PUZZLE 10

¹b	u	s	²h

³e g y p t i a n

⁴b

⁵l a z a r u ⁶s

⁷f

i

⁸t e n

⁹c a r p e n t e r

¹⁰f e d s e a n

PUZZLE 11

			1 J											
			U											
			D		2 B								3 J	
			4 G	I	A	N	T	S		5 C	A	L	E	B
			E		B								R	
			S		Y								I	
					L			6 J					C	
	7 S				O		8 D	E	B	O	R	A	H	
9 G	I	D	E	O	N			S					O	
	N				I			S						
	A			10 S	A	M	U	E	L					
	I				N									

PUZZLE 12

							1 Y							
							E							
		2 E					A						3 C	
		L					4 R	E	5 H	O	B	O	A	M
	6 P	I	L	L	7 A	R	S	■	E				I	
		S			R			8 S	A	M	S	O	N	
		H			K				V					
9 S	T	A	F	F				10 D	E	L	I	L	A	H
									N					

PUZZLE 13

1 R
E
B
3 W I S D O M **4** M
I
5 E V **2** J
E
K Z
A E
C
7 D
8 H A N N A H **9** R U T H
A
V I
10 S O L O M O N
I
D

PUZZLE 14

1 A
G
A
2 Z **3** G **4** J
5 I D O L **6** G O M E R
P L Z
7 P H I L I S T I N E S
O A B
8 E S T H E R **9** D E
A T **10** S A U L
H H V
I
D

PUZZLE 15

Across:
1. FIFTH
4. LOT
6. ORPAH
9. LIGHT
10. ONE / ONEBED

Down:
2. TWO
3. JOSCH
5. THRD
7. ARMMOR
8. STONE
10. ONENES

(grid letters)

1 F I F T H
2 W (down)
4 L O 5 T
3 J
6 O R P A H 7 A
8 S C R
9 L I G H T H M
L R O
D R
10 O N E B E D
N N
E E
S D

PUZZLE 16

1 W
I 2 J
3 T W O
C N
H A
4 S
A
T U
7 P H I L I S T I A 6 A 5 B
A A R
8 C R E
9 J A V E L I N 10 S W O R D A
V N D
E

PUZZLE 17

Across:
4. NATHAN
6. JESUS
7. CAMEL
10. SOLOMON

Down:
1. DANIEL
2. SO
3. URIAH
5. NABAL
8. JONAH
9. JOSAB

Grid letters:
- 1 D, A
- 2 S, O
- 3 U, R, I, A(H)
- 4 N A T H A N
- 5 N, B
- 6 J E S U S
- 7 C A M E L
- 8 J O N A H
- 9 J, A, B
- 10 S O L O M O N
- S A L O M
- A B

PUZZLE 18

Grid letters:
- 1 A B D N E G O
- 2 A B S A L O M
- 3 B E R N A T I T
- 4 D A R I U
- 5 F R N A E
- 6 N E B U C H A D N E Z Z A R
- 7 J E S U S
- 8 C Y R U S
- 9 N E H E M I A H
- S

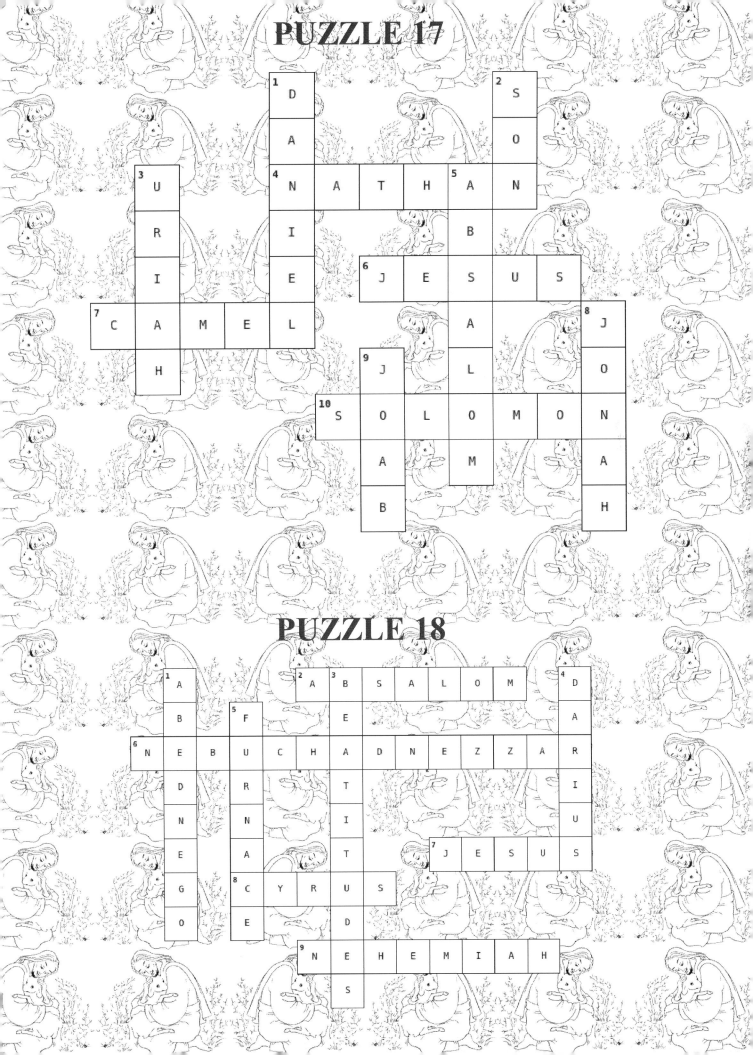

PUZZLE 19

1 CARPENTER
2 FISHING
3 PILATE
4 GOD
5 NICODEMUS
6 SATAN
7 BAPTIST
8 DEMONS
9 LEGION

PUZZLE 20

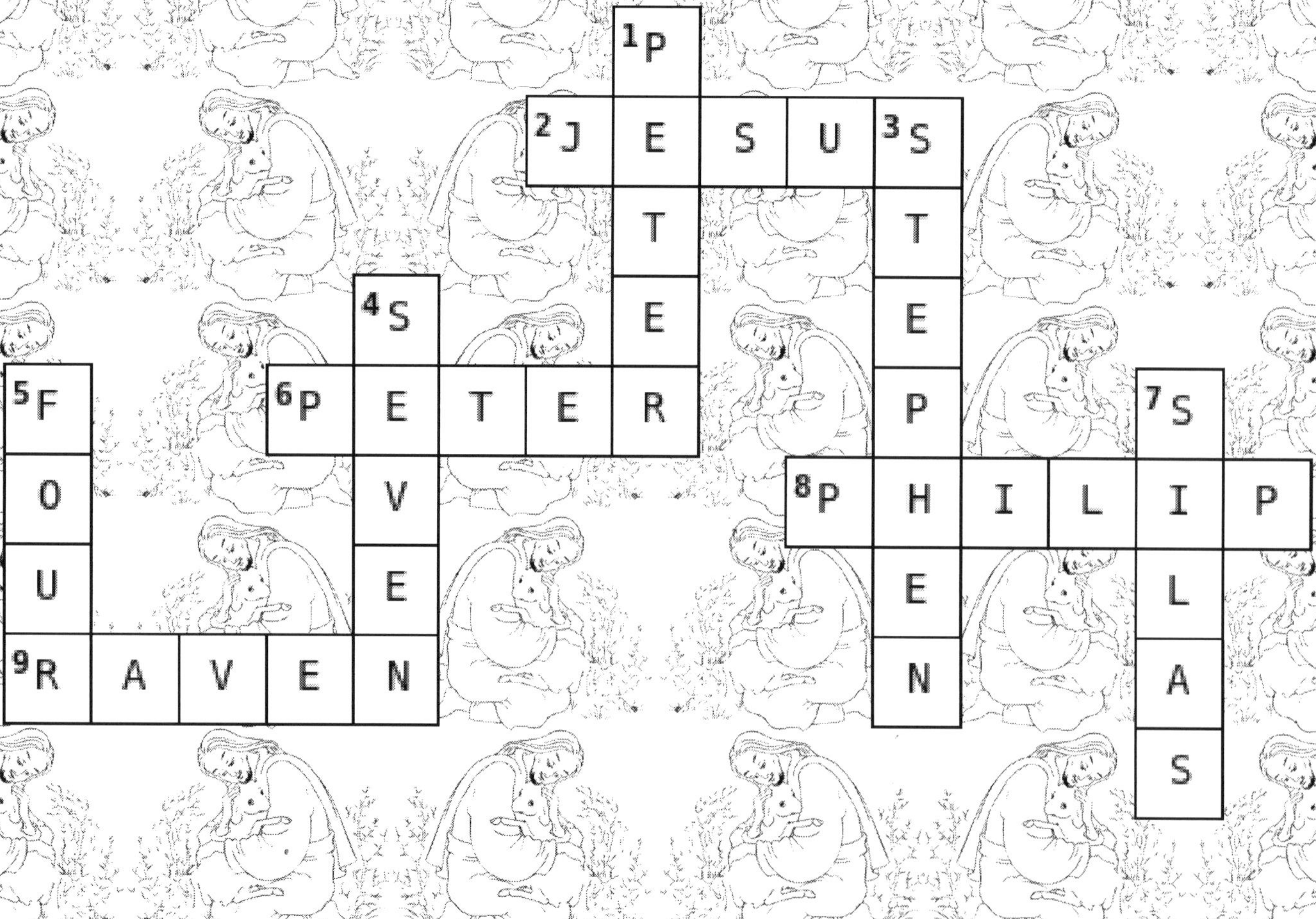

1 PETER
2 JESUS
3 STEPHEN
4 SEVEN
5 FOUR
6 PETER
7 SILAS
8 PHILIP
9 RAVEN

WELCOME
TO
CRYPTOGRAM PUZZLES

Each phrase has been encrypted/encoded by simple letter substitution. To solve the puzzles, the kid need to guess the letters that have been replaced by trial and error methods.

TIPS

- The most common letters in the English language are E, T, A, O, I, N. These letters occur often in words.
- Start with single letter words. Common single letter words are "A" and "I".
- Look for common letter combinations, like "TH" and "SH".
- The most common two-letter words are: OF, TO, IN, IS, IT, AS, HE, BE, BY, ON, OR, and AT.
- AND and THE lead the list of three-letter words with FOR, HIS, NOT, BUT, YOU, ARE, HER, HAD, CAN and HOW coming after.
- Look out for words that start and end with the same letter like this pattern "OAVO". This is usually the word "THAT".
- All English language words usually have at least one vowel.
- Watch out for repeated letters. Only a few letters are usually ever repeated twice in a word: RR, LL, NN, MM, FF, OO, EE and fewer of these are in small words.
- Look for words with apostrophe. Such words are mostly contraction words like "CAN'T", "WON'T", "DIDN'T", "YOU'RE", "YOU'LL".
- If you ever hit a snag while solving the puzzles, the hint and answers in the book can come in handy.

IS RKXNPHK'M THHJHK

_ _ *BROTHER'S* _ _ _ _ _ _

EUC EBAEU OUHDD SHMC QIA GBCC

THE _

HD DTN NSNANUDT TPCV

_ _ *THE* _ _ _ _ _ _ _ _ _ _ _ _

JDF BQICS QFRSICM JDF BQICS

THE _ _ _ _ _ _ _ _ _ _ _ _ _ *THE* _ _ _ _ _

XU GZN FCOJ IE UIBP GNNGZ

_ _ _ _ _ _ _ _ _ _ _ _ _ _ *TEETH*

OIW, RXEBV IBR GO DOXXU

_ _ _ _ *DRINK* _ _ _ _ _ _ _ _ _ _

AH SGXX EW ALV KGWUQZV

__ ____ __ ___ *WAYSIDE*

YGGU TY XLED

FEET __ ____

FJZM HP WIK OHPWVKPW

_ ___ __ ___ *OINTMENT*

YB VYNV VWILYBVY FDVLY

__ *THAT* _____ _____

PQS JRNC TD ULJH RNC QTNSF

___ ____ __ ____ *AND* _____

ZVI DKBT JE BJT

THE ____ __ ___

GBZHAGNW XGQQHV XFGQOZ UVP PAHVP

_ _____ _____ _____ ITS _____

BDZL TBTMF SK SVL HBTUQVSLY

____ _ ____ __ ___ SLAUGHTER

RSKOOYNXLZ RVXHLQ IXHV LZUB

_ MILLSTONE _____ ____ ____

BS DSIV DSEJBTXJP

__ MOVE _____

LVNGN IP WOLVIWX WNJ FWCNG LVN PFW

THERE __ _____ ___ _____ ___ ___

ZHQ EADZDGY LG ZHQ ESBB

THE _____ __ THE ____

M YBTCC WT DEMB

_ _____ __ *BEAR*

N WSNJS QHHSCYVU

_ _____ *OFFERING*

GQBPNKT DN CTKLT OX ZVB FKEQGTX VB CBBQN

_ _____ __ _____ __ ___ _____ __ *KEEPS*

H WPCK AJ MIY MPXYW

_ *SIGN* __ ___ _____

CJUZ-EGYEG FUZAG

_ _____ *SWORD*

W OBMTJ TDPMUF MU YKJ CMHZJDUJXX

_ *VOICE* _____ __ ___ _____

D SMOA GI CJUUE'C XOMQJGIK

_ WOLF __ _____ _____

UMWAEHK XJ JERD

_____ __ FIRE

DVZAJIT NKHJBR ZI VXOK

_____ _____ __ HOME

URGB RE VGCS URZRYNK

____ __ MANY _____

IYYK NI MSTG

____ __ CLAY

YLGHC CHA GEES YLGHC

FIGHT ___ ____ FIGHT

SZO JYJOXUDAHI UDJOJ AT V TJVTZH

___ _____ *THERE* __ _ _____

HQ ZFD DEZVU BWCD

__ *THE* _____ ____

XTTI SCRCONLCH

GOOD _____

AWVYXU SJIV AXWVT

HARDEN ____ _____

FP SFB LUQPN CX OFP NSBTD, DUPN CX OFP NSBTD

__ ___ _____ __ ___ _____ ____ __ ___ *SWORD*

EJ SFO SCEJZBEJP TL YJ OXO

__ ___ _____ __ __ *EYE*

OT SIQ AQDOTTOTD GCM SIQ GPJU

__ ___ _____ ___ ___ *WORD*

UWO YIA BUA KGJUBN LYVVAE

___ *ARE* ___ _____ _____

SME ETMOM XM SBQTE

___ _____ __ *LIGHT*

UCAAC SWKU TLCYLA

_____ *FROM* _____

RJMP JA FJWPQ GD CYP BJJC JA VRR PMGR

____ __ _____ __ *THE* ____ __ ___ ____

CTEF UTPQ WFNDALTPQ RB UTPQBFCS

____ ____ _____ __ *YOURSELF*

NEV TMBF VMO RIJB PG PXBET ERMVB

___ DOES ___ ____ __ _____ _____

_____

HZXR ZNP OZTTPY JIV LPD ZNP OKCGPX

____ ___ CALLED ___ ___ ___ _____

_____

YQ XJGO IQX OZJ FEKCJH

__ ____ ___ ___ WICKED

_____

GHNEJGL GPX QGBPZ NEP OQG

_____ ___ _____ THE ___

_____

SEVRH XDOHY PHZDEH A ZATT

_____ _____ _____ _ FALL

_____

CXS HVXY EVXZU JN VYAUY

PUT ____ _____ __ _____

_____

BWWX AZI LNK BJAFF TQZI

____ ___ ___ _____ *FIND*

FYMZN RJN ZST MET FYSHB RJN CJHBT

_____ ___ ___ *AND* _____ ___ _____

OXH JAAO AN OXH BUOOHJ

THE ____ __ *THE* _____

XQC KZAUAX AK FAJJAIY ERX XQC GJCKQ AK FCLO

THE _____ __ _____ ___ *THE* _____ __ ____

GDJ VRTJF OU FZY ZF KJRGD

THE _____ __ ___ __ _____

JCOWO PCUH

JESUS ____

FXI RHSF QS RQG HT IFIEZLY YHSI HZ BXEHTF DITOT QOE YQEG

___ ____ __ ___ __ _____ ____ __ _____ _____ *OUR* ____

KHRTA ICFGS KXCF AGHXRBE

_____ *COMES* ____ _____

EFM VZ VUYT PG EUQKO, XFK PG SQNOK

___ __ *WALK* __ _____ ___ __ _____

B MK DZX UMP MRN DZX DYIDZ MRN DZX GBOX

_ __ ___ *WAY* ___ ___ _____ ___ ___ ____

EFNMVFI JR TIDU FVMN

_____ __ ____ *EVIL*

IVCE XF MGVF KQL JXZ KQVPL RZEQK

____ __ ____ ___ ___ _____ *BREAD*

Thank you so much for purchasing this book and making it this far in the book!

I greatly appreciate the time your kid is taking to solve the puzzles in this book. As a small publisher, knowing that your kid is having fun solving the puzzles and getting all the mental profit means a lot to me.

If you have 60 seconds, hearing your honest feedback on Amazon would mean the world to me. It does wonders for the book, and I love hearing about your kid's experience with the book.

How to leave a feedback:

1. Open your camera app or QR code Scanner.
2. Point your mobile device at the QR code below
3. The review page will appear in your web browser.

Or
Visit: funsided.com/BAB

WELCOME
TO
CRYPTOGRAM PUZZLES
SOLUTIONS

IS RKXNPHK'M THHJHK

MY BROTHER'S KEEPER

EUC EBAEU OUHDD SHMC QIA GBCC

THE TRUTH SHALL MAKE YOU FREE

HD DTN NSNANUDT TPCV

AT THE ELEVENTH HOUR

JDF BQICS QFRSICM JDF BQICS

THE BLIND LEADING THE BLIND

XU GZN FCOJ IE UIBP GNNGZ

BY THE SKIN OF YOUR TEETH

OIW, RXEBV IBR GO DOXXU

EAT, DRINK AND BE MERRY

AH SGXX EW ALV KGWUQZV

TO FALL BY THE WAYSIDE

YGGU TY XLED

FEET OF CLAY

FJZM HP WIK OHPWVKPW

A FLY IN THE OINTMENT

YB VYNV VWILYBVY FDVLY

HE THAT TOUCHETH PITCH

PQS JRNC TD ULJH RNC QTNSF

THE LAND OF MILK AND HONEY

ZVI DKBT JE BJT

THE LAND OF NOD

GBZHAGNW XGQQHV XFGQOZ UVP PAHVP

A LEOPARD CANNOT CHANGE ITS SPOTS

BDZL TBTMF SK SVL HBTUQVSLY

LIKE A LAMB TO THE SLAUGHTER

R SKOOYNXLZ RVXHLQ IXHV LZUB

A MILLSTONE AROUND YOUR NECK

BS DSIV DSEJBTXJP

TO MOVE MOUNTAINS

LVNGN IP WOLVIWX WNJ FWCNG LVN PFW

THERE IS NOTHING NEW UNDER THE SUN

ZHQ EADZDGY LG ZHQ ESBB

THE WRITING ON THE WALL

M YBTCC WT DEMB

A CROSS TO BEAR

N WSNJS QHHSCYVU

A PEACE OFFERING

G QBPNKT DN CTKLT OX ZVB FKEQGTX VB CBBQN

A PERSON IS KNOWN BY THE COMPANY HE KEEPS

HWPCK AJ MIY MPXYW

A SIGN OF THE TIMES

CJUZ-EGYEG FUZAG

A TWO-EDGED SWORD

W OBMTJ TDPMUF MU YKJ CMHZJDUJXX

A VOICE CRYING IN THE WILDERNESS

D SMOA GI CJUUE'C XOMQJGIK

A WOLF IN SHEEP'S CLOTHING

UMWAEHK XJ JERD

BAPTISM OF FIRE

DVZAJIT NKHJBR ZI VXOK

CHARITY BEGINS AT HOME

URGB RE VGCS URZRYNK

COAT OF MANY COLOURS

IYYK NI MSTG

FEET OF CLAY

YLGHC CHA GEES YLGHC

FIGHT THE GOOD FIGHT

SZO JYJOXUDAHI UDJOJ AT V TJVTZH

FOR EVERYTHING THERE IS A SEASON

HQ ZFD DEZVU BWCD

GO THE EXTRA MILE

XTTI SCRCONLCH

GOOD SAMARITAN

AWVYXU SJIV AXWVT

HARDEN YOUR HEART

FP SFB LUQPN CX OFP NSBTD, DUPN CX OFP NSBTD

HE WHO LIVES BY THE SWORD, DIES BY THE SWORD

EJ SFO SCEJZBEJP TL YJ OXO

IN THE TWINKLING OF AN EYE

OT SIQ AQDOTTOTD GCM SIQ GPJU

IN THE BEGINNING WAS THE WORD

UWO YIA BUA KGJUBN LYVVAE

HOW ARE THE MIGHTY FALLEN

SME ETMOM XM SBQTE

LET THERE BE LIGHT

UCAAC SWKU TLCYLA

MANNA FROM HEAVEN

RJMP JA FJWPQ GD CYP BJJC JA VRR PMGR

LOVE OF MONEY IS THE ROOT OF ALL EVIL

CTEF UTPQ WFNDALTPQ RB UTPQBFCS

LOVE YOUR NEIGHBOUR AS YOURSELF

NEV TMBF VMO RIJB PG PXBET ERMVB

MAN DOES NOT LIVE BY BREAD ALONE

HZXR ZNP OZTTPY JIV LPD ZNP OKCGPX

MANY ARE CALLED BUT FEW ARE CHOSEN

YQ XJGO IQX OZJ FEKCJH

NO REST FOR THE WICKED

GHNEJGL GPX QGBPZ NEP OQG

NOTHING NEW UNDER THE SUN

SEVRH XDOHY PHZDEH A ZATT

PRIDE COMES BEFORE A FALL

CXS HVXY EVXZU JN VYAUY

PUT YOUR HOUSE IN ORDER

BWWX AZI LNK BJAFF TQZI

SEEK AND YOU SHALL FIND

FYMZN RJN ZST MET FYSHB RJN CJHBT

SPARE THE ROD AND SPOIL THE CHILD

OXH JAAO AN OXH BUOOHJ

THE ROOT OF THE MATTER

XQC KZAUAX AK FAJJAIY ERX XQC GJCKQ AK FCLO

THE SPIRIT IS WILLING BUT THE FLESH IS WEAK

GDJ VRTJF OU FZY ZF KJRGD

THE WAGES OF SIN IS DEATH

JCOWO PCUH

JESUS WEPT

FXI RHSF QS RQG HT IFIEZLY YHSI HZ BXEHTF DITOT QOE YQEG

THE GIFT OF GOD IS ETERNAL LIFE IN CHRIST JESUS OUR LORD

KHRTA ICFGS KXCF AGHXRBE

FAITH COMES FROM HEARING

EFM VZ VUYT PG EUQKO, XFK PG SQNOK

FOR WE WALK BY FAITH, NOT BY SIGHT

B MK DZX UMP MRN DZX DYIDZ MRN DZX GBOX

I AM THE WAY AND THE TRUTH AND THE LIFE

EFNMVFI JR TIDU FVMN

DELIVER US FROM EVIL

IVCE XF MGVF KQL JXZ KQVPL RZEQK

GIVE US THIS DAY OUR DAILY BREAD

WELCOME TO EASY SUDOKU PUZZLES

Puzzle 1

9	4		3	5			6	8
				9		5		3
5	3	6		8				
						7		
			8	7	4	9	1	
6						4		2
4			7				5	
2	5			3	1		7	
1	7						2	

Puzzle 2

	7		1	2			3	
1	4							
8	3		7		9	2		4
3	8		9					
				8		1		
	9				1	4	6	8
9			8	6			4	1
					7		2	5
		4	2					

Puzzle 3

	1		8		5	2	4	9
2			9	1	7			
					4		5	
6		2	1		3	9		
			5				8	6
		8					1	2
9	8	6	7					
		4		5				1
	2	1			8			

Puzzle 4

9		6		7				
			2	9	8			6
	4					7		
	5	9	8		7			2
				6		9		3
							1	
			8			2	9	1
2		4	7	3		6		
	9	5	6	2			7	4

Puzzle 1

6		3		1		2		
	4		2	8				5
		5	6					9
		6			2			
	1						9	
3			1	4	6	7		
7			8			9		
5			4	2		1		7
	9	4				5		

Puzzle 2

			7		3	4		
2	4						3	5
3				4		2		
	3		6	1				4
5	6			9	4			
	2		3		7			
9				6	8	5	7	
		2			1			
	5	8	2				1	

Puzzle 3

	4				1	6	7	
			9	7				4
			6				1	2
			4		8			
4	7	6	3	1				
8	1	3		5			6	9
7			5				4	1
	6				2	7		
		8		3		2		6

Puzzle 4

			4		7			
				8				9
1	8	7			9			
	5	3	1					
8	1		7				4	
	2		8	3		9		
	9	5	6		3			
4			5				9	2
			9		4	3		5

Puzzle 1

	6		1			7		5
8			5	7		4	1	
	1			2	4			8
		6			2		5	
	4			3	5	8		2
		1				2		
	5		3	4	8			7
	3	8					4	

Puzzle 2

	9		4					
6		3	1	2		8		
		5		3			4	
4		2		9	1			5
	7	8			4	9		2
				6				
2	5				3			8
	8	6			2	7	3	
					7		5	6

Puzzle 3

	4		9	5		6	7	3
	9		1	7				8
	5	7	4	6			9	2
	7	2	3					
		5		8	9			
			5					7
8		9	6					
		4		1		9		6
					5	8		

Puzzle 4

6		4	8					2
	5		9	6	7		8	
7					2			5
8			3	7				
	3				9	5	6	
	1		6					9
9			5	3		8	2	
		5		2				6
			7			4	5	

Puzzle 1

```
. . . | . 8 2 | . 5 .
9 8 3 | . . 1 | . . 2
. 2 5 | 9 . 6 | . 3 .
------+-------+------
. 5 . | . . . | . 6 .
1 9 7 | . . . | . . .
3 6 . | 8 9 5 | . . .
------+-------+------
. 1 2 | 6 5 . | . . .
8 7 . | . . 3 | . . .
. . . | . . 8 | . . 4
```

Puzzle 2

```
. 5 . | . . . | . . .
. . 2 | 8 7 . | . 3 .
8 1 . | . . . | . 4 6
------+-------+------
3 6 8 | . 2 . | . 9 7
9 . . | 7 . 6 | 4 . .
7 . . | . . 9 | 2 6 .
------+-------+------
. . 4 | . . 2 | 3 . 1
. . . | . 1 3 | 8 . .
1 . . | . . 8 | 6 . .
```

Puzzle 3

```
8 . 6 | 1 . . | 2 9 3
5 3 . | . . . | . . 4
2 . . | . . . | 1 8 .
------+-------+------
. 5 7 | . . 8 | . 4 .
. 4 . | . . 1 | . . .
6 . 8 | . . . | . . .
------+-------+------
7 6 . | 8 . . | 3 . .
. 8 . | . . 9 | . . .
. . . | . 1 3 | 6 5 .
```

Puzzle 4

```
. . . | . . 2 | . . .
4 . . | 5 7 . | . 8 2
2 8 3 | . . 1 | . . 4
------+-------+------
5 1 . | . 6 . | . . .
. . . | 9 8 . | . 6 .
. 3 . | 1 2 . | . . .
------+-------+------
3 4 5 | 7 6 9 | . . .
8 . 2 | . . . | 6 . 7
1 . . | . 3 8 | 5 . 9
```

Puzzle 1

5	2						3	4
	7	1					2	
6					2	1		
	6	5	2	1		3		
1				3	7		6	
8	3	9				2		1
			3		5			
			8			6		
			4	2	6		5	3

Puzzle 2

4	1			5	8	9	7	
	2	3			1	5	8	
9					2			6
						4	6	
		4			9			
3			2				5	
5	3			2		6		
	9	1					4	
		6	1	3				8

Puzzle 3

9		8			1	6		5
			9	3		1	4	7
		3						
1	9			7			5	
	8	6		5				
	3		1				2	4
	2		6		7			
	7	9	8				6	
4	6	1			3			

Puzzle 4

	6		4		3	8		5
4	3		1	7				
8	7			9			4	
6		1	8				3	
	9	4	3			2	8	
		8		9				1
		3				7		
	4			5			2	
			3	7				

Grid 1

		9	6				1	
			9			5	7	
	2	1	7		8			
1		8	5	7				
	3	5			4			1
7	9		8	1				
		7		8		4		2
		2		3			6	
		4		5		8	3	7

Grid 2

	1	8			6			
6								
	5			8				3
	3				8	2		1
	4	6			1		5	9
1				2	4		7	
				4			1	2
8			1	3				4
4	7		9			5		8

Grid 3

1	3							7
			1	3				
4		6	9					
8		3			9	6	5	
	2	4					7	3
					5	8		
6	9					4		
3		2		6		7		
	1	5	2			3		

Grid 4

6		1			3	5		
7				5		2		6
8		4				7	3	
5	6				1			
1						4		
	8					6	2	1
3	4			1	2			
		8	6		9			7
9		6			5			2

Grid 1

8						7		
	1		5			3	4	8
		3					2	
			4			2	8	
7						9		
5		2	7	9	1	6	3	4
		4	2	8				6
2	5	9				8		
					5	4	1	

Grid 2

8		3			9	1		
6	2		4					
1	9						3	
	5	6	8	4	3	7	1	2
			7					9
	8	7			5	4		
				1				
3				8			2	7
				5				

Grid 3

							2	5
		4			8	3		1
1	3	6			7	9	4	
	2					4		
3						7		9
4		9					3	2
8		7		6	3	2	5	4
				7		1	6	3
		3		5	4			

Grid 4

	1			3	2	4		
6	9	3	5				2	8
5					7	3	6	1
8				6				2
			7	9				6
1	7		2		3			9
3						6	1	
								4
9		4		7			2	3

Puzzle 1

	7		8	6		1	9	
4			5	3	7	6	8	2
8	2		4		9			
			6		3		4	9
6	3		9		5	8	7	
7	9		1		8	3		
	5	7	3	9	1	4	6	8
9	6				4	7	1	3
3	4	1	7		6	9	2	5

Puzzle 2

4				5		3	1	6
	6						5	2
	5			6		8		
			3	7		1	6	4
		3		2	8	9		
						2		8
	7	8	4					
	1		2					
	3	2	5		9	4		1

Puzzle 3

		2	4		7			8
			2	1	6		4	
		9	5	3	8	7	1	
					1			
5	2	6						9
	4	1	7	2	9	5		
		5						6
						3		7
		3	9	6	2			1

Puzzle 4

1		3					8	
	2		4	8		6		3
		5		3	9		7	
	5					7	4	
7			4		5	3		
	8						9	
4		2		7		5	3	
			6		3		1	
		1			4	8		

Grid 1

	2			6				9
	8		4	5	9			1
9	5		3	7	2	8	6	4
7	9	8		2		4		3
3	1	2	9	8	4		7	5
5		4	7		3	2	9	8
				4	6	1	3	
		6		9	8	5	4	7
2	4	5	1	3	7	9	8	

Grid 2

	6		7			2	4	
		9			3	5	6	8
								3
		2		6				
5	4	7		8	2			6
							3	2
8	9		2	3			7	5
				7	5			
	7		8		6	3	2	9

Grid 3

			1		4	7	5	
				8			1	4
	4			7				
	7	8		3	9			
		3		8			7	
9				6			3	
	9	4			5	3		
	3	5		2			8	
8		7		4		1		

Grid 4

			4		2		7	
		9		1	5	8		3
1	4	6		3	7	9		
		4					3	
	9		1				5	
	5	7		4		1		
						7		
4	7		3	2	9			6
	6	1	7					

Puzzle 1

5					1			7
1	8			5				4
	4	7		2			5	
		1		7	5	6		
	3			8		4		5
	2		3			8		
					8	5		2
3	5						8	
	1			9		3		

Puzzle 2

1	6						3	
7		5	1	3				8
	8		9		6	1		5
6		1	8	4			5	2
		7		2				6
	5	8	6					
			5	6		4		1
8		6		9				
	4				1			

Puzzle 3

	5	7				4		
		8	1		2	7		
1	4							
7	8							2
4				2	9	8		3
	2	5	6		7			
9		1				5		
					5	3	4	
5					3		6	8

Puzzle 4

4								5
5			4	2	8		6	
1	2	7	3			9		4
3	1		6	4		8		
		4	8		2	1		
		8			1			
8	7			6				
9	5					6	4	
			2			3		9

Puzzle 1

6					8	4		1
			9	2			6	
		5	1	4	6		9	
9	3		4		7			
	6	2						
		1		8	2		4	3
		4		6		5	8	
						6		
2	7	6					3	

Puzzle 2

	2		6		8		1	
7	6	4		3				
			5		9			
							3	9
4	3	5		1			7	
6		1	3					
3	4						8	
	5		1		4	9		3
						5		7

Puzzle 3

	9							
	1	7		5	3		9	
4		2	8	9				5
3	8	4						
	2		7					6
5				3	2	4		1
		9		7	1		6	
	5							2
	6	8			5	7	3	9

Puzzle 4

2		3	4	1	5			
	4	7	3				2	
5			7	8	2		9	
		9	6		8			
		1	5	2	7			
7		2						
3		4				6	8	1
		8		4				
		5			3	2	4	9

Puzzle 1

9	6	1	4	5	3		2	
		7	6				1	3
						6		
5	9	3	7					
			9					
			3	6		8		9
				8				7
	3	8	2		9			6
1		6						2

Puzzle 2

5		9			7	2	6	
		3	6	1	9	5	4	
							1	3
1			6		9	4		
4			3		1			
			8	7				
			9	5				6
			7		6			
	3		1	8		7		

Puzzle 3

	5		7	2		3	6	
6			5		3	1		2
1				9		7		
			1		7			
			2	5		6		3
	4	5	6		9	8		1
5								6
	2	1	4	6	5		8	
			3			4		

Puzzle 4

		2	7	8		5	3	
1				3	9		7	
			4	1	5		2	
		6				8	9	4
2				6	1	7		
3	7	9		5		6		
	9						8	
4		5				3		9
								5

Puzzle 1 (top-left)

	7				6			
	1					4		3
				1	3	2		9
	3	8				7	2	
7	4	2					9	6
5	9	1	6				4	8
	5	4	3				1	7
1	6		4		9	5		
8	2	7						

Puzzle 2 (top-right)

8			1	5		6	9	3
6			2			7	1	5
7								
9	7	8	5				2	
	6		8					
2	1			7	6			
		7		2			6	1
		3				8	7	9
			8	1			5	

Puzzle 3 (bottom-left)

		1	5	3				8
7	4		9	2				
		3			6	7		
	5	7						
		6		7	5	1	9	4
					9	3		5
3			6	9				
1	6				7	4	2	
5	7		3		2	8		

Puzzle 4 (bottom-right)

	9	1		4			8	
		8						6
5	6			9	8	7	4	
1			6		2			8
		9				6		
		6				3	5	
	1	7			9	8		5
		2	3	8		4		
8			7		5	1		9

Grid 1

	9					2	1	
4	1				9	8		
		8			7		3	
	5	2		7	8			4
8				3				2
7								
		5	7	4	3		2	
	8			5	6	1	4	
		4						

Grid 2

3				9	5		6	
			4			2	1	
6		4	2		7		9	
2			9				7	6
5			8				3	
		6	3					1
8				4				
4			6		3	8		9
	3	9		2	8	6	4	7

Grid 3

			8	6	7	4		2
					9	1		8
	5	7	4			3		
1				8	5	6		
4								
	7		6			2	3	
	8				6	5		
		6	7			9		
5		4			3			

Grid 4

5		6	2		4	8		7
		1					5	9
6	2		1				3	
	8			2			4	1
7		3			9	5	2	
1	6		4	8				5
8		2	5					
		9			6		8	

Puzzle 1

	7	1		2	6		9	
							3	7
		2				1		4
			4	3				
6	2	8	9				4	3
3						9		
	4			1			5	
		3	6	7	5	4		9
	5		2					1

Puzzle 2

	2							9
	5	6	4			8	7	
4								
	6		5	3	1	9	2	
	3	2	7			4		
		1	2					7
9			3			2		
	7	8		2	4	3	9	5
2	4			5	8			6

Puzzle 3

3				6			4	7
			9				8	5
5		4	7	3		9		
	4	9	1					
6	5	1			2		7	
	3		5	7				4
			4					6
	2				7			
	7			1		5	9	8

Puzzle 4

4					1	9		2
			4	3	7			6
			2	6	9	8	3	
8								
6	1		9		2			3
2			7					
7		8	6	2			1	9
		1		9			2	8
				7		4		

WELCOME TO EASY SUDOKU PUZZLES SOLUTIONS

Grid 1

9	4	1	3	5	7	2	6	8
7	8	2	1	9	6	5	4	3
5	3	6	4	8	2	1	9	7
8	1	4	2	6	9	7	3	5
3	2	5	8	7	4	9	1	6
6	9	7	5	1	3	4	8	2
4	6	9	7	2	8	3	5	1
2	5	8	9	3	1	6	7	4
1	7	3	6	4	5	8	2	9

Grid 2

5	7	9	1	2	4	8	3	6
1	4	2	6	3	8	9	5	7
8	3	6	7	5	9	2	1	4
3	8	1	9	4	6	5	7	2
4	6	7	5	8	2	1	9	3
2	9	5	3	7	1	4	6	8
9	2	3	8	6	5	7	4	1
6	1	8	4	9	7	3	2	5
7	5	4	2	1	3	6	8	9

Grid 3

7	1	3	8	6	5	2	4	9
2	4	5	9	1	7	6	3	8
8	6	9	3	2	4	1	5	7
6	5	2	1	8	3	9	7	4
1	9	7	5	4	2	3	8	6
4	3	8	6	7	9	5	1	2
9	8	6	7	3	1	4	2	5
3	7	4	2	5	6	8	9	1
5	2	1	4	9	8	7	6	3

Grid 4

9	2	6	1	7	4	8	3	5
5	3	7	2	9	8	1	4	6
1	4	8	3	5	6	7	2	9
3	5	9	8	1	7	4	6	2
4	7	1	5	6	2	9	8	3
6	8	2	9	4	3	5	1	7
7	6	3	4	8	5	2	9	1
2	1	4	7	3	9	6	5	8
8	9	5	6	2	1	3	7	4

Grid 1

6	7	3	9	1	5	2	8	4
9	4	1	2	8	3	6	7	5
8	2	5	6	7	4	3	1	9
4	5	6	7	9	2	8	3	1
2	1	7	5	3	8	4	9	6
3	8	9	1	4	6	7	5	2
7	6	2	8	5	1	9	4	3
5	3	8	4	2	9	1	6	7
1	9	4	3	6	7	5	2	8

Grid 2

1	8	5	7	2	3	4	6	9
2	4	7	9	8	6	1	3	5
3	9	6	1	4	5	2	8	7
7	3	9	6	1	2	8	5	4
5	6	1	8	9	4	7	2	3
8	2	4	3	5	7	6	9	1
9	1	3	4	6	8	5	7	2
6	7	2	5	3	1	9	4	8
4	5	8	2	7	9	3	1	6

Grid 3

3	4	9	8	2	1	6	7	5
6	2	1	9	7	5	3	8	4
5	8	7	6	4	3	9	1	2
2	9	5	4	6	8	1	3	7
4	7	6	3	1	9	5	2	8
8	1	3	2	5	7	4	6	9
7	3	2	5	9	6	8	4	1
9	6	4	1	8	2	7	5	3
1	5	8	7	3	4	2	9	6

Grid 4

3	6	9	4	5	7	1	2	8
5	4	2	3	1	8	7	6	9
1	8	7	2	6	9	5	3	4
9	5	3	1	4	2	8	7	6
8	1	6	7	9	5	2	4	3
7	2	4	8	3	6	9	5	1
2	9	5	6	8	3	4	1	7
4	3	8	5	7	1	6	9	2
6	7	1	9	2	4	3	8	5

Grid 1

9	6	4	1	8	3	7	2	5
8	2	3	5	7	6	4	1	9
5	1	7	9	2	4	6	3	8
2	8	5	4	6	9	3	7	1
3	7	6	8	1	2	9	5	4
1	4	9	7	3	5	8	6	2
4	9	1	6	5	7	2	8	3
6	5	2	3	4	8	1	9	7
7	3	8	2	9	1	5	4	6

Grid 2

8	9	1	4	7	6	5	2	3
6	4	3	1	2	5	8	7	9
7	2	5	8	3	9	6	4	1
4	6	2	7	9	1	3	8	5
1	7	8	3	5	4	9	6	2
5	3	9	2	6	8	4	1	7
2	5	7	6	4	3	1	9	8
9	8	6	5	1	2	7	3	4
3	1	4	9	8	7	2	5	6

Grid 3

1	4	8	9	5	2	6	7	3
2	9	6	1	7	3	4	5	8
3	5	7	4	6	8	1	9	2
6	7	2	3	4	1	5	8	9
4	3	5	7	8	9	2	6	1
9	8	1	5	2	6	3	4	7
8	1	9	6	3	4	7	2	5
5	2	4	8	1	7	9	3	6
7	6	3	2	9	5	8	1	4

Grid 4

6	9	4	8	5	3	1	7	2
2	5	1	9	6	7	3	8	4
7	8	3	1	4	2	6	9	5
8	6	9	3	7	5	2	4	1
4	3	7	2	1	9	5	6	8
5	1	2	6	8	4	7	3	9
9	4	6	5	3	1	8	2	7
3	7	5	4	2	8	9	1	6
1	2	8	7	9	6	4	5	3

Grid 1

6	4	1	3	8	2	9	5	7
9	8	3	5	7	1	6	4	2
7	2	5	9	4	6	1	3	8
2	5	8	1	3	7	4	6	9
1	9	7	2	6	4	3	8	5
3	6	4	8	9	5	7	2	1
4	1	2	6	5	9	8	7	3
8	7	9	4	2	3	5	1	6
5	3	6	7	1	8	2	9	4

Grid 2

6	5	7	3	4	1	8	2	9
4	9	2	6	8	7	1	3	5
8	1	3	2	9	5	7	4	6
3	6	8	1	2	4	5	9	7
9	2	5	7	3	6	4	1	8
7	4	1	8	5	9	2	6	3
5	8	4	9	6	2	3	7	1
2	7	6	5	1	3	9	8	4
1	3	9	4	7	8	6	5	2

Grid 3

8	7	6	1	4	5	2	9	3
5	3	1	9	8	2	7	6	4
2	9	4	3	7	6	1	8	5
3	5	7	2	6	8	9	4	1
9	4	2	5	3	1	8	7	6
6	1	8	4	9	7	5	3	2
7	6	5	8	2	4	3	1	9
1	8	3	6	5	9	4	2	7
4	2	9	7	1	3	6	5	8

Grid 4

9	5	7	8	4	2	3	1	6
4	6	1	3	5	7	9	8	2
2	8	3	6	9	1	7	5	4
5	1	8	4	7	6	2	9	3
7	2	4	9	8	3	1	6	5
6	3	9	1	2	5	4	7	8
3	4	5	7	6	9	8	2	1
8	9	2	5	1	4	6	3	7
1	7	6	2	3	8	5	4	9

Puzzle 1

5	2	8	1	6	9	7	3	4
4	7	1	5	8	3	9	2	6
6	9	3	7	4	2	1	8	5
7	6	5	2	1	8	3	4	9
1	4	2	9	3	7	5	6	8
8	3	9	6	5	4	2	7	1
2	8	6	3	9	5	4	1	7
3	5	4	8	7	1	6	9	2
9	1	7	4	2	6	8	5	3

Puzzle 2

4	1	3	6	5	8	9	7	2
6	7	2	3	9	1	5	8	4
9	8	5	4	7	2	1	3	6
8	2	7	5	1	3	4	6	9
1	5	4	8	6	9	7	2	3
3	6	9	2	4	7	8	5	1
5	3	8	9	2	4	6	1	7
2	9	1	7	8	6	3	4	5
7	4	6	1	3	5	2	9	8

Puzzle 3

9	4	8	7	2	1	6	3	5
6	5	2	9	3	8	1	4	7
7	1	3	5	6	4	2	8	9
1	9	4	3	7	2	8	5	6
2	8	6	4	5	9	7	1	3
5	3	7	1	8	6	9	2	4
8	2	5	6	4	7	3	9	1
3	7	9	8	1	5	4	6	2
4	6	1	2	9	3	5	7	8

Puzzle 4

1	6	9	4	2	3	8	7	5
4	3	5	1	7	8	6	9	2
8	7	2	5	6	9	1	4	3
6	5	1	8	4	2	9	3	7
7	9	4	3	5	1	2	8	6
3	2	8	7	9	6	4	5	1
5	1	3	2	8	4	7	6	9
9	4	7	6	1	5	3	2	8
2	8	6	9	3	7	5	1	4

Grid 1

4	7	9	3	6	5	2	1	8
6	8	3	9	2	1	5	7	4
5	2	1	7	4	8	6	9	3
1	4	8	5	7	3	9	2	6
2	3	5	6	9	4	7	8	1
7	9	6	8	1	2	3	4	5
3	6	7	1	8	9	4	5	2
8	5	2	4	3	7	1	6	9
9	1	4	2	5	6	8	3	7

Grid 2

3	1	8	4	5	6	9	2	7
6	9	2	7	1	3	4	8	5
7	5	4	2	8	9	1	6	3
5	3	7	6	9	8	2	4	1
2	4	6	3	7	1	8	5	9
1	8	9	5	2	4	3	7	6
9	6	3	8	4	5	7	1	2
8	2	5	1	3	7	6	9	4
4	7	1	9	6	2	5	3	8

Grid 3

1	3	9	8	5	4	2	6	7
2	8	7	6	1	3	5	4	9
4	5	6	7	9	2	1	3	8
8	7	3	4	2	9	6	5	1
5	2	4	1	8	6	9	7	3
9	6	1	3	7	5	8	2	4
6	9	8	5	3	7	4	1	2
3	4	2	9	6	1	7	8	5
7	1	5	2	4	8	3	9	6

Grid 4

6	2	1	9	7	3	5	8	4
7	9	3	8	5	4	2	1	6
8	5	4	1	2	6	7	3	9
5	6	2	4	9	1	8	7	3
1	3	7	2	6	8	4	9	5
4	8	9	5	3	7	6	2	1
3	4	5	7	1	2	9	6	8
2	1	8	6	4	9	3	5	7
9	7	6	3	8	5	1	4	2

8	2	5	1	4	3	7	6	9
9	1	7	5	6	2	3	4	8
4	6	3	8	7	9	1	2	5
3	9	1	4	5	6	2	8	7
7	4	6	3	2	8	9	5	1
5	8	2	7	9	1	6	3	4
1	3	4	2	8	7	5	9	6
2	5	9	6	1	4	8	7	3
6	7	8	9	3	5	4	1	2

8	7	3	2	6	9	1	4	5
6	2	5	4	3	1	9	7	8
1	9	4	5	7	8	2	3	6
9	5	6	8	4	3	7	1	2
4	3	1	7	2	6	8	5	9
2	8	7	1	9	5	4	6	3
5	6	2	9	1	7	3	8	4
3	1	9	6	8	4	5	2	7
7	4	8	3	5	2	6	9	1

9	7	8	3	4	1	6	2	5
2	5	4	6	9	8	3	7	1
1	3	6	5	2	7	9	4	8
7	2	1	9	3	5	4	8	6
3	6	5	4	8	2	7	1	9
4	8	9	7	1	6	5	3	2
8	9	7	1	6	3	2	5	4
5	4	2	8	7	9	1	6	3
6	1	3	2	5	4	8	9	7

7	1	8	6	3	2	4	9	5
6	9	3	5	1	4	2	8	7
5	4	2	9	8	7	3	6	1
8	3	9	1	6	5	7	4	2
4	2	5	7	9	8	1	3	6
1	7	6	2	4	3	8	5	9
3	5	7	4	2	9	6	1	8
2	8	1	3	5	6	9	7	4
9	6	4	8	7	1	5	2	3

5	7	3	8	6	2	1	9	4
4	1	9	5	3	7	6	8	2
8	2	6	4	1	9	5	3	7
1	8	5	6	7	3	2	4	9
6	3	4	9	2	5	8	7	1
7	9	2	1	4	8	3	5	6
2	5	7	3	9	1	4	6	8
9	6	8	2	5	4	7	1	3
3	4	1	7	8	6	9	2	5

4	8	9	7	5	2	3	1	6
3	6	1	8	9	4	7	5	2
2	5	7	3	6	1	8	4	9
8	2	5	9	3	7	1	6	4
1	4	3	6	2	8	9	7	5
7	9	6	1	4	5	2	3	8
9	7	8	4	1	6	5	2	3
5	1	4	2	8	3	6	9	7
6	3	2	5	7	9	4	8	1

1	5	2	4	9	7	6	3	8
3	7	8	2	1	6	9	4	5
4	6	9	5	3	8	7	1	2
9	3	7	6	5	1	2	8	4
5	2	6	8	4	3	1	7	9
8	4	1	7	2	9	5	6	3
2	1	5	3	7	4	8	9	6
6	9	4	1	8	5	3	2	7
7	8	3	9	6	2	4	5	1

1	4	3	7	5	6	2	8	9
9	2	7	1	4	8	6	5	3
8	6	5	2	3	9	4	7	1
3	5	6	9	1	2	7	4	8
7	1	9	4	8	5	3	6	2
2	8	4	3	6	7	1	9	5
4	9	2	8	7	1	5	3	6
5	7	8	6	2	3	9	1	4
6	3	1	5	9	4	8	2	7

Grid 1

4	2	3	8	6	1	7	5	9
6	8	7	4	5	9	3	2	1
9	5	1	3	7	2	8	6	4
7	9	8	6	2	5	4	1	3
3	1	2	9	8	4	6	7	5
5	6	4	7	1	3	2	9	8
8	7	9	5	4	6	1	3	2
1	3	6	2	9	8	5	4	7
2	4	5	1	3	7	9	8	6

Grid 2

3	6	8	7	5	9	2	4	1
7	2	9	1	4	3	5	6	8
1	5	4	6	2	8	7	9	3
9	3	2	4	6	1	8	5	7
5	4	7	3	8	2	9	1	6
6	8	1	5	9	7	4	3	2
8	9	6	2	3	4	1	7	5
2	1	3	9	7	5	6	8	4
4	7	5	8	1	6	3	2	9

Grid 3

3	8	6	1	9	4	7	5	2
7	2	9	3	5	8	6	1	4
5	4	1	6	7	2	8	9	3
6	7	8	5	3	9	2	4	1
4	5	3	2	8	1	9	7	6
9	1	2	4	6	7	5	3	8
2	9	4	8	1	5	3	6	7
1	3	5	7	2	6	4	8	9
8	6	7	9	4	3	1	2	5

Grid 4

3	8	5	4	9	2	6	7	1
7	2	9	6	1	5	8	4	3
1	4	6	8	3	7	9	2	5
6	1	4	9	5	8	2	3	7
2	9	3	1	7	6	4	5	8
8	5	7	2	4	3	1	6	9
9	3	2	5	6	1	7	8	4
4	7	8	3	2	9	5	1	6
5	6	1	7	8	4	3	9	2

Grid 1

5	6	2	8	4	1	9	3	7
1	8	3	7	5	9	2	6	4
9	4	7	6	2	3	1	5	8
8	9	1	4	7	5	6	2	3
7	3	6	9	8	2	4	1	5
4	2	5	3	1	6	8	7	9
6	7	4	1	3	8	5	9	2
3	5	9	2	6	4	7	8	1
2	1	8	5	9	7	3	4	6

Grid 2

1	6	9	2	5	8	7	3	4
7	2	5	1	3	4	6	9	8
3	8	4	9	7	6	1	2	5
6	3	1	8	4	7	9	5	2
4	9	7	3	2	5	8	1	6
2	5	8	6	1	9	3	4	7
9	7	2	5	6	3	4	8	1
8	1	6	4	9	2	5	7	3
5	4	3	7	8	1	2	6	9

Grid 3

2	5	7	3	9	8	4	1	6
6	9	8	1	4	2	7	3	5
1	4	3	7	5	6	2	8	9
7	8	9	4	3	1	6	5	2
4	1	6	5	2	9	8	7	3
3	2	5	6	8	7	1	9	4
9	3	1	8	6	4	5	2	7
8	6	2	9	7	5	3	4	1
5	7	4	2	1	3	9	6	8

Grid 4

4	8	6	1	9	7	2	3	5
5	3	9	4	2	8	7	6	1
1	2	7	3	5	6	9	8	4
3	1	5	6	4	9	8	2	7
7	9	4	8	3	2	1	5	6
2	6	8	5	7	1	4	9	3
8	7	3	9	6	4	5	1	2
9	5	2	7	1	3	6	4	8
6	4	1	2	8	5	3	7	9

Grid 1

6	9	3	5	7	8	4	2	1
1	4	7	9	2	3	8	6	5
8	2	5	1	4	6	3	9	7
9	3	8	4	1	7	2	5	6
4	6	2	3	9	5	7	1	8
7	5	1	6	8	2	9	4	3
3	1	4	7	6	9	5	8	2
5	8	9	2	3	1	6	7	4
2	7	6	8	5	4	1	3	9

Grid 2

5	2	9	6	7	8	3	1	4
7	6	4	2	3	1	8	9	5
1	8	3	5	4	9	7	2	6
2	7	8	4	5	6	1	3	9
4	3	5	9	1	2	6	7	8
6	9	1	3	8	7	4	5	2
3	4	6	7	9	5	2	8	1
8	5	7	1	2	4	9	6	3
9	1	2	8	6	3	5	4	7

Grid 3

8	9	5	1	6	4	2	7	3
6	1	7	2	5	3	8	9	4
4	3	2	8	9	7	6	1	5
3	8	4	5	1	6	9	2	7
9	2	1	7	4	8	3	5	6
5	7	6	9	3	2	4	8	1
2	4	9	3	7	1	5	6	8
7	5	3	6	8	9	1	4	2
1	6	8	4	2	5	7	3	9

Grid 4

2	9	3	4	1	5	8	7	6
8	4	7	3	9	6	1	2	5
5	1	6	7	8	2	4	9	3
4	5	9	6	3	8	7	1	2
6	8	1	5	2	7	9	3	4
7	3	2	9	4	1	5	6	8
3	7	4	2	5	9	6	8	1
9	2	8	1	6	4	3	5	7
1	6	5	8	7	3	2	4	9

Grid 1

9	6	1	4	5	3	7	2	8
8	4	7	6	9	2	5	1	3
3	2	5	8	1	7	6	9	4
5	9	3	7	4	8	2	6	1
6	8	4	9	2	1	3	7	5
7	1	2	3	6	5	8	4	9
2	5	9	1	8	6	4	3	7
4	3	8	2	7	9	1	5	6
1	7	6	5	3	4	9	8	2

Grid 2

5	1	9	4	3	7	2	6	8
8	2	3	6	1	9	5	4	7
7	6	4	5	2	8	1	3	9
1	7	6	2	9	5	4	8	3
4	5	8	3	6	1	9	7	2
3	9	2	8	7	4	6	5	1
2	4	7	9	5	3	8	1	6
9	8	1	7	4	6	3	2	5
6	3	5	1	8	2	7	9	4

Grid 3

4	5	9	7	2	1	3	6	8
6	8	7	5	4	3	1	9	2
1	3	2	8	9	6	7	5	4
2	6	3	1	8	7	5	4	9
9	1	8	2	5	4	6	7	3
7	4	5	6	3	9	8	2	1
5	7	4	9	1	8	2	3	6
3	2	1	4	6	5	9	8	7
8	9	6	3	7	2	4	1	5

Grid 4

9	4	2	7	8	6	5	3	1
1	5	8	2	3	9	4	7	6
7	6	3	4	1	5	9	2	8
5	1	6	3	2	7	8	9	4
2	8	4	9	6	1	7	5	3
3	7	9	8	5	4	6	1	2
6	9	1	5	4	3	2	8	7
4	2	5	1	7	8	3	6	9
8	3	7	6	9	2	1	4	5

Puzzle 1

3	7	9	2	4	6	8	5	1
2	1	6	9	5	8	4	7	3
4	8	5	7	1	3	2	6	9
6	3	8	1	9	4	7	2	5
7	4	2	8	3	5	1	9	6
5	9	1	6	2	7	3	4	8
9	5	4	3	8	2	6	1	7
1	6	3	4	7	9	5	8	2
8	2	7	5	6	1	9	3	4

Puzzle 2

8	4	2	1	5	7	6	9	3
6	3	9	2	4	8	7	1	5
7	5	1	6	9	3	2	8	4
9	7	8	5	3	4	1	2	6
3	6	5	8	1	2	9	4	7
2	1	4	9	7	6	5	3	8
5	8	7	3	2	9	4	6	1
1	2	3	4	6	5	8	7	9
4	9	6	7	8	1	3	5	2

Puzzle 3

6	2	1	7	5	3	9	4	8
7	4	5	9	2	8	6	3	1
8	9	3	1	4	6	7	5	2
9	5	7	4	3	1	2	8	6
2	3	6	8	7	5	1	9	4
4	1	8	2	6	9	3	7	5
3	8	2	6	9	4	5	1	7
1	6	9	5	8	7	4	2	3
5	7	4	3	1	2	8	6	9

Puzzle 4

7	9	1	5	4	6	2	8	3
4	2	8	1	7	3	5	9	6
5	6	3	2	9	8	7	4	1
1	4	5	6	3	2	9	7	8
3	7	9	8	5	4	6	1	2
2	8	6	9	1	7	3	5	4
6	1	7	4	2	9	8	3	5
9	5	2	3	8	1	4	6	7
8	3	4	7	6	5	1	2	9

3	9	7	5	8	4	2	1	6
4	1	6	3	2	9	8	7	5
5	2	8	6	1	7	4	3	9
6	5	2	1	7	8	3	9	4
8	4	1	9	3	5	7	6	2
7	3	9	4	6	2	5	8	1
1	6	5	7	4	3	9	2	8
9	8	3	2	5	6	1	4	7
2	7	4	8	9	1	6	5	3

3	2	8	1	9	5	7	6	4
7	9	5	4	3	6	2	1	8
6	1	4	2	8	7	3	9	5
2	8	3	9	5	1	4	7	6
5	7	1	8	6	4	9	3	2
9	4	6	3	7	2	5	8	1
8	6	2	7	4	9	1	5	3
4	5	7	6	1	3	8	2	9
1	3	9	5	2	8	6	4	7

3	9	1	8	6	7	4	5	2
6	4	2	5	3	9	1	7	8
8	5	7	4	2	1	3	6	9
1	2	3	9	8	5	6	4	7
4	6	5	3	7	2	8	9	1
9	7	8	6	1	4	2	3	5
7	8	9	1	4	6	5	2	3
2	3	6	7	5	8	9	1	4
5	1	4	2	9	3	7	8	6

5	9	6	2	3	4	8	1	7
3	4	1	7	6	8	2	5	9
2	7	8	9	1	5	4	6	3
6	2	4	1	5	7	9	3	8
9	8	5	6	2	3	7	4	1
7	1	3	8	4	9	5	2	6
1	6	7	4	8	2	3	9	5
8	3	2	5	9	1	6	7	4
4	5	9	3	7	6	1	8	2

Grid 1

4	7	1	3	2	6	5	9	8
5	6	9	1	8	4	2	3	7
8	3	2	5	9	7	1	6	4
7	9	5	4	3	8	6	1	2
6	2	8	9	5	1	7	4	3
3	1	4	7	6	2	9	8	5
2	4	7	8	1	9	3	5	6
1	8	3	6	7	5	4	2	9
9	5	6	2	4	3	8	7	1

Grid 2

3	2	7	8	1	5	6	4	9
1	5	6	4	9	2	8	7	3
4	8	9	6	7	3	1	5	2
7	6	4	5	3	1	9	2	8
5	3	2	7	8	9	4	6	1
8	9	1	2	4	6	5	3	7
9	1	5	3	6	7	2	8	4
6	7	8	1	2	4	3	9	5
2	4	3	9	5	8	7	1	6

Grid 3

3	9	2	8	6	5	1	4	7
1	6	7	9	2	4	3	8	5
5	8	4	7	3	1	9	6	2
7	4	9	1	8	6	2	5	3
6	5	1	3	4	2	8	7	9
2	3	8	5	7	9	6	1	4
9	1	3	4	5	8	7	2	6
8	2	5	6	9	7	4	3	1
4	7	6	2	1	3	5	9	8

Grid 4

4	3	6	8	5	1	9	7	2
9	8	2	4	3	7	1	5	6
1	7	5	2	6	9	8	3	4
8	9	3	5	1	6	2	4	7
6	1	7	9	4	2	5	8	3
2	5	4	7	8	3	6	9	1
7	4	8	6	2	5	3	1	9
5	6	1	3	9	4	7	2	8
3	2	9	1	7	8	4	6	5

WELCOME TO HARD SUDOKU PUZZLES

Grid 1

3					4	5		
	2	5	7	3	8			9
	4		1		6	3		
			8			9	5	
4	7							1
5		8		4		2	7	
7			4					
	6	2					4	
				6				8

Grid 2

	4			3	2	7		
3				6	9	2		
		2		5			1	3
9			6	2			3	
	3			1				7
2	8							
			3	8	4			
				7				
	6	3			1	4		8

Grid 3

1	9							8
	2		9				5	
		4			1	7		
3						6		
2	4	7		5				3
8							4	
		5		8		9		
					4	2	6	
			6	7	9		8	

Grid 4

7			3		8			9
3	5	4				1		
	9					2		
			1		6		2	3
			4		2	6		
6			9	8				
			3				9	
2			5		4			
	4		2	6		8	1	

Puzzle 1 (top-left)

		5					2	7
2		1		5				4
				4				
			5				8	3
					7	9	4	
4		2			9			
9		6			3			
	7	3			5	4	9	
8				9			7	5

Puzzle 2 (top-right)

			6		8	5		
5		6				9	2	
			5	1	2		3	6
4	2			7	9			8
9	7		4	8		2	1	3
	1	8		5		4	9	7
		9			7			5
		2	3					9
			9	6			8	2

Puzzle 3 (bottom-left)

5			2		7	4	9	6
3		2	5	6		7	8	1
		9			4	2	3	5
6	3	7		5		8	2	9
8			7	9		6	4	3
2	9	4		8	3	5	1	7
1			3		6	9	7	2
	7		9	2	5	1		
	2			7	8	3	5	4

Puzzle 4 (bottom-right)

6							7	1
		4	6		5	2	3	8
						6		
4		8			3			
	6		9			4		3
		5	1	6				
			7			8		5
7				3			4	
	1		4		9	3		

Puzzle 1

				6	3	4		
	1		7	8				
8		6					2	
		7	6		4			5
5	9					8		
				9				7
		9		2	1			
	2		4			9		8
4	5				6			2

Puzzle 2

	2				6	4		
					4		1	
				2		6	5	
	5							
3						5	9	6
4	1		6		5	7		
5				4		1		
8		4	9		1		3	
			5	8		9		4

Puzzle 3

		4	2	8		9		
					9	7	1	
7		9			5			
		3		5	1			9
			9			3		
		8			2		5	4
8	9			7				6
	2							
	3		1		4			8

Puzzle 4

1	3	6	8		4			2
4	5	9	7	2	1			
	2			3		4	1	5
6	4				7		2	3
		2	5					
8	7	3	1					4
			2		6	8	5	
			4	7			3	9
	8				5	6		1

Puzzle 1

		4	7		1			
5	1	7	4		2	8		
3		9			6			
9							4	
	4	8	1		9		3	
	5	3				1		
1	9			4				
8	3	6						5
					5	3	8	

Puzzle 2

6	8						5	
			8		7			
7	1			4	5		6	8
	4			8		2		
	6			3				4
	5		1			4		
5							9	4
			6		2	1		
	9		7			8		

Puzzle 3

5				7	8			2
					9		8	7
		2		1	3	4	5	
7		8			1			
	6		8		2		1	
		9			4			
6							2	
2	1							5
			2	4			7	

Puzzle 4

	5	1	3		7		8	
				2			4	9
	2		9				7	
5	9	4						
6		2	8	5		9	1	
		8	2				5	1
2				3			9	
		9	5	7		6		

Puzzle 1

9			7		2	8		5
		4					6	
		8	4	6			1	9
			5					6
6		1	2					
8		5				2		7
4		7	9	2				
1		6	3	8	5			
				7				8

Puzzle 2

	5		9					7
8	3	7	6					5
1	2				8			6
5	8			6	2	9	4	
	7		1		9	5		
	9	1	8			3		
	1							
		8						3
			4		5			

Puzzle 3

				7	4			1
		9	1	2				
7	4	1			3			6
2								
		4	2		8	3		5
5			9					8
	7		5			4		
			4	3			1	
			7		9	8	5	

Puzzle 4

			9			2		
					1	4	6	
	4	7					9	
3		2		9			1	
						6		2
		8		5		9		
8				4		1	2	
	2	4	7	8	9	5		
	3			1	5		8	

Grid 1

5	2				1	6		7
			4			3		
					6	2		
	3		1			9	4	6
	1				8	7		3
	6		9				2	
	9		3		4			
					9	1	6	2
					2		3	

Grid 2

	6			8			5	
	4	2	9	1			7	6
3			7				4	
4		7			8	6		
	2	6				5	8	
8		5			7	4	9	
6	7						1	
			3		1			
	5		8				2	

Grid 3

		5	3	1		8		
		2			4			7
3								
	5							
			8		5	6	7	
		8		7		3	9	
	8	7	9		3	2	1	
			1	6	7		8	
				5	8	7		3

Grid 4

			2	5	7			
		5	8	3				
				1	4	3		
	3	9	1			4	6	
1								7
4	6					1	8	
8								
	4	1			5			8
	9			6	8		1	

Puzzle 1

7	2		6			8		4
9								
	5	8			2	1		
	6		8					5
1			2			4		
	9	4		5	6	7		
					8		7	6
		2	4	6			8	
			3			5		

Puzzle 2

					1	8		
				2				4
	6		3	4		2	7	
	5		4			1		
							9	
9	1							
	2	4		9		7		
1			2	7	8	9	4	
	8			1		6		

Puzzle 3

		1						7
6	8	9						3
		7		4				2
	2		1	9	6	8		4
8								
		6	7				2	
9			8		1		4	5
	6		4			9	7	
			3					8

Puzzle 4

	7		9	8	2			
		1						
3	5		6				8	
			2	1			7	8
		8	7					
6			9	8	3		4	
	6				2		1	
		4					2	3
	2			3		6		

Puzzle 1

		9		7	8			4
			2			8	7	
8			5		6		9	3
		4		3			8	
	8	2				1	3	
	5	3	8			9	4	
4	3	6				5		8
2		8				3		
	7	1	6	8				

Puzzle 2

				5		3		
							1	
	8	6	2	4				5
7	3		9			1		
2						8		
	6	8				4		9
			7	9	4			6
			3		8	7		
	4			1			9	3

Puzzle 3

	6	7	2	4			1	
				5	8		4	
4		8		3	6	5		
							8	
		1		6	3			
9				8				7
	4					6		5
	3		6	2	4			
6							2	4

Puzzle 4

			6	1	4		5	
	3	9	5	8				2
		1		3			4	8
5	4	7						
1			8			9	6	
	8					1		5
	1							
3							2	7
7				9				

Puzzle 1

8						4	7	3
						2		
9		4			2			
		3	2	9	7			1
		9						
1	8			6	5			
3	9	2	5			1		
							4	
4		1		8	9			6

Puzzle 2

	8		9	4		2	5	
	4	5	3			6		1
2								
	2	9		1			3	6
		7				9		
5	6			9				
			8		6		1	
4	7				1			
3		6		5			7	

Puzzle 3

		9		1				
	2						4	5
	4			5		7		9
						3		1
	3		7		4	6	8	
		2	1				9	
2					1	4		7
	1			3		9	5	
8				4	5			3

Puzzle 4

	2	5	3				8	7
			8				2	
7					4	3		
	7				8		4	5
			3					
	9	8				2		6
5			6		2			
			1		5	6		
		1				9		2

Puzzle 1

		2	1		4			
1								
	3	4	9					6
		6		5				
	5					6	3	8
	8			2	1	7	5	
					7		6	3
3	1		5			2	8	
		7	8			4		

Puzzle 2

	9			2				7
		6				2		
					5	9		3
			9	7		5	3	
9	3		1	5			6	
5	7		3		4			9
	8						9	
			4			1		2
	4	9		1			8	

Puzzle 3

					3	2	9	4
				2		8		1
8	2			7	1			
7			4			6	3	
				8				7
			3					2
3						9	2	
	9							5
4		5					1	6

Puzzle 4

			6	2			8	
3	8	6						
		2	8	3				9
7			1	9	4	2		8
		1	3					7
			5	7		9		1
		3		4	9			
			8			5		
8	7	9	2				1	6

WELCOME TO HARD SUDOKU PUZZLES SOLUTION

Puzzle 1

3	8	1	2	9	4	5	6	7
6	2	5	7	3	8	4	1	9
9	4	7	1	5	6	3	8	2
2	3	6	8	1	7	9	5	4
4	7	9	6	2	5	8	3	1
5	1	8	9	4	3	2	7	6
7	9	3	4	8	1	6	2	5
8	6	2	5	7	9	1	4	3
1	5	4	3	6	2	7	9	8

Puzzle 2

6	4	5	1	3	2	7	8	9
3	1	8	7	6	9	2	4	5
7	9	2	4	5	8	6	1	3
9	5	1	6	2	7	8	3	4
4	3	6	8	1	5	9	2	7
2	8	7	9	4	3	1	5	6
1	7	9	3	8	4	5	6	2
8	2	4	5	7	6	3	9	1
5	6	3	2	9	1	4	7	8

Puzzle 3

1	9	6	7	2	5	4	3	8
7	2	8	9	4	3	1	5	6
5	3	4	8	6	1	7	2	9
3	5	1	4	9	8	6	7	2
2	4	7	1	5	6	8	9	3
8	6	9	2	3	7	5	4	1
6	7	5	3	8	2	9	1	4
9	8	3	5	1	4	2	6	7
4	1	2	6	7	9	3	8	5

Puzzle 4

7	1	2	3	4	8	5	6	9
3	5	4	6	2	9	1	8	7
8	9	6	7	1	5	2	3	4
4	7	8	1	5	6	9	2	3
1	3	9	4	7	2	6	5	8
6	2	5	9	8	3	7	4	1
5	6	7	8	3	1	4	9	2
2	8	1	5	9	4	3	7	6
9	4	3	2	6	7	8	1	5

Grid 1

6	4	5	9	3	8	1	2	7
2	9	1	7	5	6	8	3	4
3	8	7	1	4	2	5	6	9
7	1	9	5	2	4	6	8	3
5	6	8	3	1	7	9	4	2
4	3	2	8	6	9	7	5	1
9	5	6	4	7	3	2	1	8
1	7	3	2	8	5	4	9	6
8	2	4	6	9	1	3	7	5

Grid 2

2	3	1	6	9	8	5	7	4
5	8	6	7	3	4	9	2	1
7	9	4	5	1	2	8	3	6
4	2	3	1	7	9	6	5	8
9	7	5	4	8	6	2	1	3
6	1	8	2	5	3	4	9	7
1	6	9	8	2	7	3	4	5
8	5	2	3	4	1	7	6	9
3	4	7	9	6	5	1	8	2

Grid 3

5	8	1	2	3	7	4	9	6
3	4	2	5	6	9	7	8	1
7	6	9	8	1	4	2	3	5
6	3	7	4	5	1	8	2	9
8	1	5	7	9	2	6	4	3
2	9	4	6	8	3	5	1	7
1	5	8	3	4	6	9	7	2
4	7	3	9	2	5	1	6	8
9	2	6	1	7	8	3	5	4

Grid 4

6	5	3	8	4	2	9	7	1
9	7	4	6	1	5	2	3	8
8	2	1	3	9	7	6	5	4
4	9	8	2	7	3	5	1	6
1	6	7	9	5	8	4	2	3
2	3	5	1	6	4	7	8	9
3	4	6	7	2	1	8	9	5
7	8	9	5	3	6	1	4	2
5	1	2	4	8	9	3	6	7

Grid 1

9	7	5	2	6	3	4	8	1
2	1	4	7	8	9	6	5	3
8	3	6	1	4	5	7	2	9
3	8	7	6	1	4	2	9	5
5	9	1	3	7	2	8	4	6
6	4	2	5	9	8	3	1	7
7	6	9	8	2	1	5	3	4
1	2	3	4	5	7	9	6	8
4	5	8	9	3	6	1	7	2

Grid 2

9	2	8	1	5	6	4	7	3
6	5	3	7	9	4	8	1	2
7	4	1	3	2	8	6	5	9
2	6	5	8	7	9	3	4	1
3	8	7	4	1	2	5	9	6
4	1	9	6	3	5	7	2	8
5	9	6	2	4	3	1	8	7
8	7	4	9	6	1	2	3	5
1	3	2	5	8	7	9	6	4

Grid 3

1	5	4	2	8	7	9	6	3
3	8	2	4	6	9	7	1	5
7	6	9	3	1	5	4	8	2
2	4	3	6	5	1	8	7	9
5	7	6	9	4	8	3	2	1
9	1	8	7	3	2	6	5	4
8	9	1	5	7	3	2	4	6
4	2	5	8	9	6	1	3	7
6	3	7	1	2	4	5	9	8

Grid 4

1	3	6	8	5	4	9	7	2
4	5	9	7	2	1	3	8	6
7	2	8	6	3	9	4	1	5
6	4	5	9	8	7	1	2	3
9	1	2	5	4	3	7	6	8
8	7	3	1	6	2	5	9	4
3	9	4	2	1	6	8	5	7
5	6	1	4	7	8	2	3	9
2	8	7	3	9	5	6	4	1

Grid 1

6	8	4	7	3	1	9	5	2
5	1	7	4	9	2	8	6	3
3	2	9	8	5	6	7	1	4
9	6	1	5	7	3	2	4	8
7	4	8	1	2	9	5	3	6
2	5	3	6	8	4	1	7	9
1	9	5	3	4	8	6	2	7
8	3	6	2	1	7	4	9	5
4	7	2	9	6	5	3	8	1

Grid 2

6	8	4	1	3	9	7	5	2
9	2	5	8	6	7	4	1	3
7	1	3	2	4	5	9	6	8
3	4	9	5	7	8	6	2	1
1	6	7	4	2	3	5	8	9
8	5	2	9	1	6	3	4	7
5	7	6	3	8	1	2	9	4
4	3	8	6	9	2	1	7	5
2	9	1	7	5	4	8	3	6

Grid 3

5	9	1	4	7	8	3	6	2
4	3	6	5	2	9	1	8	7
8	7	2	6	1	3	4	5	9
7	4	8	3	5	1	2	9	6
3	6	5	8	9	2	7	1	4
1	2	9	7	6	4	5	3	8
6	5	4	1	8	7	9	2	3
2	1	7	9	3	6	8	4	5
9	8	3	2	4	5	6	7	1

Grid 4

9	5	1	3	4	7	2	8	6
8	7	3	1	6	2	5	4	9
4	2	6	9	8	5	1	7	3
5	9	4	7	3	1	8	6	2
1	8	7	6	2	9	4	3	5
6	3	2	8	5	4	9	1	7
7	4	8	2	9	6	3	5	1
2	6	5	4	1	3	7	9	8
3	1	9	5	7	8	6	2	4

Grid 1

9	6	3	7	1	2	8	4	5
7	1	4	8	5	9	3	6	2
2	5	8	4	6	3	7	1	9
3	9	2	5	4	7	1	8	6
6	7	1	2	9	8	4	5	3
8	4	5	6	3	1	2	9	7
4	8	7	9	2	6	5	3	1
1	2	6	3	8	5	9	7	4
5	3	9	1	7	4	6	2	8

Grid 2

4	5	6	9	2	3	1	8	7
8	3	7	6	4	1	2	9	5
1	2	9	5	7	8	4	3	6
5	8	3	7	6	2	9	4	1
2	7	4	1	3	9	5	6	8
6	9	1	8	5	4	3	7	2
7	1	5	3	9	6	8	2	4
9	4	8	2	1	7	6	5	3
3	6	2	4	8	5	7	1	9

Grid 3

3	5	2	6	7	4	9	8	1
6	8	9	1	2	5	7	3	4
7	4	1	8	9	3	5	2	6
2	6	8	3	5	7	1	4	9
9	1	4	2	6	8	3	7	5
5	3	7	9	4	1	2	6	8
1	7	3	5	8	6	4	9	2
8	9	5	4	3	2	6	1	7
4	2	6	7	1	9	8	5	3

Grid 4

5	1	3	9	6	4	2	7	8
2	8	9	3	7	1	4	6	5
6	4	7	5	2	8	3	9	1
3	5	2	4	9	6	8	1	7
4	9	1	8	3	7	6	5	2
7	6	8	1	5	2	9	4	3
8	7	5	6	4	3	1	2	9
1	2	4	7	8	9	5	3	6
9	3	6	2	1	5	7	8	4

Grid 1

5	2	4	8	3	1	6	9	7
9	8	6	4	2	7	3	1	5
3	7	1	5	9	6	2	8	4
2	3	8	1	7	5	9	4	6
4	1	9	2	6	8	7	5	3
7	6	5	9	4	3	8	2	1
6	9	2	3	1	4	5	7	8
8	4	3	7	5	9	1	6	2
1	5	7	6	8	2	4	3	9

Grid 2

7	6	9	2	8	4	1	5	3
5	4	2	9	1	3	8	7	6
3	1	8	7	6	5	2	4	9
4	9	7	1	5	8	6	3	2
1	2	6	4	3	9	5	8	7
8	3	5	6	2	7	4	9	1
6	7	3	5	4	2	9	1	8
2	8	4	3	9	1	7	6	5
9	5	1	8	7	6	3	2	4

Grid 3

9	7	5	3	1	2	8	6	4
8	6	2	5	9	4	1	3	7
3	1	4	7	8	6	9	5	2
7	5	1	6	3	9	4	2	8
4	3	9	8	2	5	6	7	1
6	2	8	4	7	1	3	9	5
5	8	7	9	4	3	2	1	6
2	4	3	1	6	7	5	8	9
1	9	6	2	5	8	7	4	3

Grid 4

3	1	4	2	5	7	8	9	6
9	2	5	8	3	6	7	4	1
6	8	7	9	1	4	3	5	2
7	3	9	1	8	2	4	6	5
1	5	8	6	4	3	9	2	7
4	6	2	5	7	9	1	8	3
8	7	6	4	2	1	5	3	9
2	4	1	3	9	5	6	7	8
5	9	3	7	6	8	2	1	4

Grid 1

7	2	1	6	3	5	8	9	4
9	4	3	7	8	1	6	5	2
6	5	8	9	4	2	1	3	7
2	6	7	8	9	4	3	1	5
1	8	5	2	7	3	4	6	9
3	9	4	1	5	6	7	2	8
4	3	9	5	1	8	2	7	6
5	1	2	4	6	7	9	8	3
8	7	6	3	2	9	5	4	1

Grid 2

2	4	5	7	9	1	8	6	3
3	9	7	8	2	6	5	1	4
8	6	1	5	3	4	2	7	9
6	5	3	9	4	7	1	2	8
4	7	8	1	5	2	3	9	6
9	1	2	6	8	3	4	5	7
5	2	4	3	6	9	7	8	1
1	3	6	2	7	8	9	4	5
7	8	9	4	1	5	6	3	2

Grid 3

2	4	1	9	3	5	6	8	7
6	8	9	2	1	7	4	5	3
5	3	7	6	4	8	1	9	2
7	2	5	1	9	6	8	3	4
8	9	3	5	2	4	7	1	6
4	1	6	7	8	3	5	2	9
9	7	2	8	6	1	3	4	5
3	6	8	4	5	2	9	7	1
1	5	4	3	7	9	2	6	8

Grid 4

4	7	6	1	9	8	2	3	5
8	9	1	3	2	5	4	6	7
3	5	2	6	4	7	9	8	1
9	4	5	2	1	6	3	7	8
2	3	8	7	5	4	1	9	6
6	1	7	9	8	3	5	4	2
5	6	3	4	7	2	8	1	9
1	8	4	5	6	9	7	2	3
7	2	9	8	3	1	6	5	4

Grid 1

1	2	9	3	7	8	6	5	4
3	6	5	2	4	9	8	7	1
8	4	7	5	1	6	2	9	3
6	1	4	9	3	5	7	8	2
9	8	2	4	6	7	1	3	5
7	5	3	8	2	1	9	4	6
4	3	6	7	9	2	5	1	8
2	9	8	1	5	4	3	6	7
5	7	1	6	8	3	4	2	9

Grid 2

4	7	1	6	5	9	3	2	8
9	5	2	8	3	7	6	1	4
3	8	6	2	4	1	9	7	5
7	3	4	9	8	5	1	6	2
2	1	9	4	6	3	8	5	7
5	6	8	1	7	2	4	3	9
1	2	3	7	9	4	5	8	6
6	9	5	3	2	8	7	4	1
8	4	7	5	1	6	2	9	3

Grid 3

5	6	7	2	4	9	8	1	3
2	1	3	7	5	8	9	4	6
4	9	8	1	3	6	5	7	2
3	5	6	9	7	2	4	8	1
8	7	1	4	6	3	2	5	9
9	2	4	5	8	1	3	6	7
1	4	2	8	9	7	6	3	5
7	3	5	6	2	4	1	9	8
6	8	9	3	1	5	7	2	4

Grid 4

2	7	8	6	1	4	3	5	9
4	3	9	5	8	7	6	1	2
6	5	1	2	3	9	7	4	8
5	4	7	9	6	1	2	8	3
1	2	3	8	7	5	9	6	4
9	8	6	3	4	2	1	7	5
8	1	5	7	2	3	4	9	6
3	9	4	1	5	6	8	2	7
7	6	2	4	9	8	5	3	1

Grid 1

8	2	6	9	5	1	4	7	3
7	1	5	6	3	4	2	9	8
9	3	4	8	7	2	6	1	5
5	4	3	2	9	7	8	6	1
2	6	9	3	1	8	7	5	4
1	8	7	4	6	5	9	3	2
3	9	2	5	4	6	1	8	7
6	7	8	1	2	3	5	4	9
4	5	1	7	8	9	3	2	6

Grid 2

6	8	1	9	4	7	2	5	3
7	4	5	3	2	8	6	9	1
2	9	3	1	6	5	4	8	7
8	2	9	5	1	4	7	3	6
1	3	7	6	8	2	9	4	5
5	6	4	7	9	3	1	2	8
9	5	2	8	7	6	3	1	4
4	7	8	2	3	1	5	6	9
3	1	6	4	5	9	8	7	2

Grid 3

5	7	9	4	1	2	8	3	6
6	2	8	3	7	9	1	4	5
3	4	1	8	5	6	7	2	9
9	6	4	5	2	8	3	7	1
1	3	5	7	9	4	6	8	2
7	8	2	1	6	3	5	9	4
2	5	3	9	8	1	4	6	7
4	1	6	2	3	7	9	5	8
8	9	7	6	4	5	2	1	3

Grid 4

6	2	5	3	1	9	4	8	7
3	1	4	8	7	6	5	2	9
7	8	9	5	2	4	3	6	1
2	7	3	9	6	8	1	4	5
4	5	6	2	3	1	7	9	8
1	9	8	4	5	7	2	3	6
5	3	7	6	9	2	8	1	4
9	4	2	1	8	5	6	7	3
8	6	1	7	4	3	9	5	2

Grid 1

5	6	2	1	3	4	8	7	9
1	9	8	7	6	5	3	4	2
7	3	4	9	8	2	5	1	6
4	7	6	3	5	8	9	2	1
2	5	1	4	7	9	6	3	8
9	8	3	6	2	1	7	5	4
8	4	5	2	9	7	1	6	3
3	1	9	5	4	6	2	8	7
6	2	7	8	1	3	4	9	5

Grid 2

8	9	3	4	2	1	6	5	7
4	5	6	7	3	9	2	1	8
2	1	7	6	8	5	9	4	3
6	2	4	8	9	7	5	3	1
9	3	8	1	5	2	7	6	4
5	7	1	3	6	4	8	2	9
1	8	2	5	7	3	4	9	6
3	6	5	9	4	8	1	7	2
7	4	9	2	1	6	3	8	5

Grid 3

1	5	7	8	6	3	2	9	4
9	6	3	5	2	4	8	7	1
8	2	4	9	7	1	5	6	3
7	1	8	4	5	2	6	3	9
2	3	9	1	8	6	4	5	7
5	4	6	3	9	7	1	8	2
3	7	1	6	4	5	9	2	8
6	9	2	7	1	8	3	4	5
4	8	5	2	3	9	7	1	6

Grid 4

9	1	7	4	6	2	3	8	5
3	8	6	9	1	5	7	2	4
5	4	2	8	3	7	1	6	9
7	6	5	1	9	4	2	3	8
4	9	1	3	2	8	6	5	7
2	3	8	5	7	6	9	4	1
1	5	3	6	4	9	8	7	2
6	2	4	7	8	1	5	9	3
8	7	9	2	5	3	4	1	6

WELCOME TO
WORD SCRAMBLE

dvaid	=_____	eenrpt	=_____	ied	=_____
eev	=_____	tsana	=_____	hsojau	=_____
socsr	=_____	thifa	=_____	oaotlggh	=_____
rak	=_____	ulhlaejlah	=_____	ujelsao	=_____
lorgy	=_____	ngcaheirp	=_____	nnmikas	=_____
bsesl	=_____	relniatove	=_____	lehl	= shoaann =_____
tsre	=_____	bcnanarzdzeehu	=_____		
ocurrritnese	=_____	reble	=_____	gcera	=_____
amsoht	=_____	oventcna	=_____	ngeal	=_____
atrmahaan	=_____	htera	=_____	dog	=_____
ussje	=_____	scveeaernper	=_____	eryystm	=_____
asitn	=_____	derma	=_____	lkwa	=_____
wal	=_____	iesemne	=_____	ztiaepb	=_____
jdeusg	=_____	jonh	=_____	lief	=_____
asmleu	=_____	droecr	=_____	abab	=_____
oethppr	=_____	lghti	=_____	elptem	=_____
gkni	=_____	elthebmeh	=_____	pmasl	=_____
oiwsmd	=_____	rchchu	=_____	idmknog	=_____
lheas	=_____	peeca	=_____	bnrioaw	=_____
vleedbo	=_____	oerdmfe	=_____	aypr	=_____
osmes	=_____	mbahara	=_____	speastol	=_____
xelie	=_____	maonetnte	=_____	nsi	=_____
laup	=_____	lewgkndoe	=_____	nsoomol	=_____
truht	=_____	eoph	=_____	aadm	=_____
ipsert	=_____	nlda	=_____	trpee	=_____
anerstv	=_____	rhseet	=_____	smdoen	=_____
esetrd	=_____	ltarceabne	=_____	hrsitc	=_____
eolgsp	=_____	pscdilei	=_____	lhoy	=_____

ilahacm	= _____	rsycu	= _____	bnjinema	= _____
sehlanko	= _____	ojshai	= _____	iel	= _____
lcusa	= _____	lisas	= _____	zrea	= _____
ievl	= _____	hetan	= _____	steh	= _____
johna	= _____	aoistb	= _____	jesma	= _____
erhest	= _____	ielxf	= _____	odneig	= _____
danoec	= _____	duje	= _____	nrweda	= _____
strebprye	= _____	heldlai	= _____	cniosoenfs	= _____
oanh	= _____	jhluhleala	= _____	aothsm	= _____
ojcba	= _____	hepeob	= _____	shdaod	= _____
eblca	= _____	aliuj	= _____	earhs	= _____
sahetn	= _____	eshba	= _____	dara	= _____
efbeil	= _____	caarhyz	= _____	eezkile	= _____
aon	= _____	msnoi	= _____	atoichn	= _____
hzitbalee	= _____	taestntem	= _____	ubenre	= _____
abeercc	= _____	rbethri	= _____	ihlilt	= _____
ieahsms	= _____	sicaa	= _____	ialelaul	= _____
lenhoiss	= _____	usculi	= _____	topitineesnadr	= _____
yacpaoespl	= _____	kuel	= _____	nana	= _____
xinrdalaae	= _____	hrtoatahs	= _____	uttis	= _____
arona	= _____	aanictsnifitoc	= _____	iantaptris	= _____
tanhnilea	= _____	leihaj	= _____	ageselitvn	= _____
daa	= _____	hojn	= _____	bbyoanl	= _____
name	= _____	termaihaa	= _____	esluma	= _____
tfig	= _____	ayarcvl	= _____	caer	= _____
reehdphs	= _____	abaelpr	= _____	eahl	= _____
nthhaato	= _____	mahci	= _____	liyad	= _____
reeba	= _____	hlceo	= _____	opihbs	= _____

seengsi	= _____	seumal	= _____	sueodx	= _____
zmiahp	= _____	oortmnydeue	= _____	onerk	= _____
atylsr	= _____	rpaeg	= _____	tneabhy	= _____
paert	= _____	umascdsa	= _____	ceaaesra	= _____
raze	= _____	rancepmau	= _____	deebr	= _____
cyeern	= _____	udjseg	= _____	ediabhsat	= _____
nda	= _____	mero	= _____	aazg	= _____
iraythat	= _____	sslpam	= _____	turh	= _____
otnadh	= _____	rreag	= _____	muemas	= _____
ehmieahn	= _____	oazr	= _____	teescsalcs ei	= _____
lgaigl	= _____	ceorihj	= _____	bhetel	= _____
hehailadppli	= _____	ibgneo	= _____	acldeoai	= _____
rnaah	= _____	oahrz	= _____	useiciltv	= _____
abegih	= _____	usseehp	= _____	amasda	= _____
hscmmaih	= _____	nbo	= _____	pbegtahhe	= _____
ahmar	= _____	sehtre	= _____	eejrzle	= _____
yhrcas	= _____	hrtezpaha	= _____	osmod	= _____
meejurlas	= _____	iaaoenssclht	= _____	dlyad	= _____
nharzeta	= _____	rhmoogar	= _____	isohhl	= _____
ymra	= _____	hasouj	= _____	sosocle	= _____
isgkn	= _____	psphoa	= _____	mnuoiic	= _____
rebsnum	= _____	eihktor	= _____	beelhmeht	= _____
oastr	= _____	ekoat	= _____	aacn	= _____
beornh	= _____	nheveni	= _____	brporves	= _____
ainn	= _____	spragmeo	= _____	oernd	= _____
jbo	= _____	cthniro	= _____	gons	= _____
rsncioechl	= _____	plpiihpi	= _____	samriaa	= _____
lsimtue	= _____	emechsh	= _____	iosdn	= _____

diaboha = _____	onoolsm = _____	kahaukkb = _____
camih = _____	titob = _____	usmael = _____
sunsnaa = _____	npheilmo = _____	hhiaja = _____
eolj = _____	hoaes = _____	nomras = _____
luhie = _____	azzuih = _____	kram = _____
seaamnsh = _____	zaah = _____	euclifr = _____
najho = _____	eamobhor = _____	oosssniacl = _____
altteosnamin = _____	zlikeee = _____	htaojm = _____
haindjoa = _____	lgbeair = _____	ijdthu = _____
rtevoinela = _____	hsaeoh = _____	hsinipaiplp = _____
cbeseaacm = _____	znaahehip = _____	samo = _____
nntaha = _____	tmyioth = _____	iatnhcrnois = _____
lhamaci = _____	moisdw = _____	aezlkei = _____
ujde = _____	emlhiac = _____	advdi = _____
ejsam = _____	cteiseaclcssiu = _____	sdesra = _____
achurb = _____	sinaagtla = _____	aunhm = _____
maiazah = _____	chaarhzie = _____	hojn = _____
arjmiehe = _____	aezr = _____	erhalpa = _____
soems = _____	ptere = _____	ustit = _____
ehizaalj = _____	so tetelaatsfcpsh = _____ o _____	usal = _____
inlead = _____	gghaai = _____	aeljih = _____
haeojsh = _____	oeduxs = _____	ukel = _____
ouajsh = _____	ailseh = _____	whtetma = _____
ahespenis = _____	eihamnhe = _____	iaihas = _____
hrebsew = _____	yacaorphp = _____	eahotlassisnn = _____

WELCOME TO WORD SCRAMBLE SOLUTION

dvaid	=	david	eenrpt	=	repent	ied	=	die
eev	=	eve	tsana	=	satan	hsojau	=	joshua
socsr	=	cross	thifa	=	faith	oaotlggh	=	golgotha
rak	=	ark	ulhlaejlah	=	hallelujah	ujelsao	=	jealous
lorgy	=	glory	ngcaheirp	=	preaching	nnmikas	=	kinsman
bsesl	=	bless	relniatove	=	revelation	lehl	=	hell
tsre	=	rest	bcnanarzdzeehu	=	nebuchadnezzar	shoaann	=	hosanna
ocurrritnese	=	resurrection	reble	=	rebel	gcera	=	grace
amsoht	=	thomas	oventcna	=	covenant	ngeal	=	angel
atrmahaan	=	maranatha	htera	=	heart	dog	=	god
ussje	=	jesus	scveeaernper	=	perseverance	eryystm	=	mystery
asitn	=	saint	derma	=	dream	lkwa	=	walk
wal	=	law	iesemne	=	enemies	ztiaepb	=	baptize
jdeusg	=	judges	jonh	=	john	lief	=	life
asmleu	=	samuel	droecr	=	record	abab	=	abba
oethppr	=	prophet	lghti	=	light	elptem	=	temple
gkni	=	king	elthebmeh	=	bethlehem	pmasl	=	psalm
oiwsmd	=	wisdom	rchchu	=	church	idmknog	=	kingdom
lheas	=	selah	peeca	=	peace	bnrioaw	=	rainbow
vleedbo	=	beloved	oerdmfe	=	freedom	aypr	=	pray
osmes	=	moses	mbahara	=	abraham	speastol	=	apostles
xelie	=	exile	maonetnte	=	atonement	nsi	=	sin
laup	=	paul	lewgkndoe	=	knowlegde	nsoomol	=	solomon
truht	=	truth	eoph	=	hope	aadm	=	adam
ipsert	=	priest	nlda	=	land	trpee	=	peter
anerstv	=	servant	rhseet	=	esther	smdoen	=	demons
esetrd	=	desert	ltarceabne	=	tabernacle	hrsitc	=	christ
eolgsp	=	gospel	pscdilei	=	disciple	lhoy	=	holy

ilahacm	=	malachi	rsycu	=	cyrus	bnjinema	=	benjamin
sehlanko	=	ashkelon	ojshai	=	josiah	iel	=	eli
lcusa	=	lucas	lisas	=	silas	zrea	=	ezra
ievl	=	levi	hetan	=	ethan	steh	=	seth
johna	=	jonah	aoistb	=	tobias	jesma	=	james
erhest	=	esther	ielxf	=	felix	odneig	=	gideon
danoec	=	deacon	duje	=	jude	nrweda	=	andrew
strebpry e	=	presbyter	heldlai	=	delilah	cniosoenfs	=	confession
oanh	=	noah	jhluhleala	=	hallelujah	aothsm	=	thomas
ojcba	=	jacob	hepeob	=	phoebe	shdaod	=	ashdod
eblca	=	caleb	aliuj	=	julia	earhs	=	asher
sahetn	=	athens	eshba	=	sheba	dara	=	arad
efbeil	=	belief	caarhyz	=	zachary	eezkile	=	ezekiel
aon	=	noa	msnoi	=	simon	atoichn	=	antioch
hzitbalee	=	elizabeth	taestntem	=	testament	ubenre	=	reuben
abeercc	=	rebecca	rbethri	=	rebirth	ihlilt	=	lilith
ieahsms	=	messiah	sicaa	=	isaac	ialelaul	=	alleluia
lenhoiss	=	holiness	usculi	=	luciu	topitineesnadr	=	
yacpaoespl	=	apocalypse	kuel	=	s	predestination	nana	
					luke		=	anna
xinrdalaae	=	alexandria	hrtoatahs	=	ashtaroth	uttis	=	titus
arona	=	aaron	aanictsnifitoc	=	sanctification	iantaptris	=	antipatris
tanhnilea	=	nathaniel	leihaj	=	elijah	ageselitvn	=	evangelist
daa	=	ada	hojn	=	john	bbyoanl	=	babylon
name	=	amen	termaihaa	=	arimathea	esluma	=	samuel
tfig	=	gift	ayarcvl	=	calvary	caer	=	acre
reehdphs	=	shepherd	abaelpr	=	parable	eahl	=	leah
nthhaato	=	anathoth	mahci	=	micah	liyad	=	lydia
reeba	=	berea	hlceo	=	chloe	opihbs	=	bishop

seengsi = genesis	seumal = samuel	sueodx = exodus
	oortmnydeue = deuteronomy	onerk = ekron
zmiahp = mizpah	rpaeg = perga	tneabhy = bethany
atehsr = lystra	umascdsa = damascus	ceaaesra = caesarea
raze = ezra	rancepmau = capernaum	deebr = derbe
cyeern = cyrene	udjseg = judges	ediabhsat = bethsaida
nda = dan	mero = rome	aazg = gaza
iraythat = thyatira	sslpam = psalms	turh = ruth
otnadh = dothan	rreag = gerar	muemas = emmaus
ehmieahn = nehemiah	oazr = zoar	teescsalcsei = ecclesiastes
lgaigl = gilgal	ceorihj = jericho	bhetel = bethel
ehailadpplih = philadelphia	ibgneo = gibeon	acldeoai = laodicea
rnaah = haran	oahrz = hazor	useiciltv = leviticus
abegih = gibeah	usseehp = ephesus	amasda = masada
hscmmaih = michmash	nbo = nob	pbegtahhe = bethphage
ahmar = ramah	sehtre = esther	eejrzle = jezreel
yhrcas = sychar	hrtezpaha = zarephath	osmod = sodom
meejurlas = jerusalem	iaaoenssclht = thessalonica	dlyad = lydda
nharzeta = nazareth	rhmoogar = gomorrah	isohhl = shiloh
ymra = myra	hasouj = joshua	sosocle = colosse
isgkn = kings	psphoa = paphos	mnuoiic = iconium
rebsnum = numbers	eihktor = kerioth	beelhmeht = bethlehem
oastr = troas	ekoat = tekoa	aacn = cana
beornh = hebron	nheveni = nineveh	brporves = proverbs
ainn = nain	spragmeo = pergamos	oernd = endor
jbo = job	cthniro = corinth	gons = song
rsncioechl = chronicles	plpiihpi = philippi	samriaa = samaria
lsimtue = miletus	emechsh = shechem	iosdn = sidon

diaboha	=	obadiah	onoolsm	=	solomon	kahaukkb	=	habakkuk
camih	=	micah	titob	=	tobit	usmael	=	samuel
sunsnaa	=	susanna	npheilmo	=	philemon	hhiaja	=	ahijah
eolj	=	joel	hoaes	=	hosea	nomras	=	romans
luhie	=	elihu	azzuih	=	uzziah	kram	=	mark
seaamnsh	=	manasseh	zaah	=	ahaz	euclifr	=	lucifer
najho	=	jonah	eamobhor	=	rehoboam	oosssniacl	=	colossians
altteosnamin	=	lamentations	zlikeee	=	ezekiel	htaojm	=	jotham
haindjoa	=	adonijah	lgbeair	=	gabriel	ijdthu	=	judith
rtevoinela	=	revelation	hsaeoh	=	hoshea	hsinipaiplp	=	philippians
cbeseaacm	=	maccabees	znaahehip	=	zephaniah	samo	=	amos
nntaha	=	nathan	tmyioth	=	timothy	iatnhcmois	=	corinthians
lhamaci	=	malachi	moisdw	=	wisdom	aezlkei	=	ezekial
ujde	=	jude	emlhiac	=	michael	advdi	=	david
ejsam	=	james	cteiseaclcssiu	=	ecclesiasticus	sdesra	=	esdras
achurb	=	baruch	sinaagtla	=	galatians	aunhm	=	nahum
maiazah	=	amaziah	chaarhzie	=	zechariah	hojn	=	john
arjmiehe	=	jeremiah	aezr	=	ezra	erhalpa	=	raphael
soems	=	moses	ptereso	=	peter	ustit	=	titus
ehizaalj	=	jahaziel	tetelaatsfcpsho	=	acts of the apostles	usal	=	saul
inlead	=	daniel	gghaai	=	haggai	aeljih	=	elijah
haeojsh	=	jehoash	oeduxs	=	exodus	ukel	=	luke
ouajsh	=	joshua	ailseh	=	elisha	whtetma	=	matthew
ahespenis	=	ephesians	eihamnhe	=	nehemiah	iaihas	=	isaiah
hrebsew	=	hebrews	yacaorphp	=	apocrypha	eahotlassisnn	=	thessalonians

Thank you so much for purchasing this book and making it this far in the book!

I greatly appreciate the time your kid is taking to solve the puzzles in this book. As a small publisher, knowing that your kid is having fun solving the puzzles and getting all the mental profit means a lot to me.

If you have 60 seconds, hearing your honest feedback on Amazon would mean the world to me. It does wonders for the book, and I love hearing about your kid's experience with the book.

How to leave a feedback:

1. Open your camera app or QR code Scanner.
2. Point your mobile device at the QR code below
3. The review page will appear in your web browser.

Or
Visit: funsided.com/BAB

Made in the USA
Las Vegas, NV
01 October 2024

96085185R00092